*An Introduction to
Sea Fishing*

An Introduction to Sea Fishing

Trevor Housby

Line Illustrations by Keith Linsell

The Crowood Press

First published in 1992 by
The Crowood Press Ltd
Ramsbury, Marlborough
Wiltshire SN8 2HR

British Library Cataloguing in Publication Data

A catalogue record for this book is available from the British Library.

ISBN 1 85223 653 1

All photographs by the author.

Dedication
To my son Russell.

Edited and designed by
D & N Publishing
DTP & Editorial Services
The Old Surgery
Crowle Road
Lambourn
Berkshire RG16 7NR

Phototypeset by FIDO Imagesetting,
Witney, Oxon

Printed and bound by Times Publishing Group,
Singapore

Contents

Introduction

Sea angling is a year round sport – as one species leaves our shores another arrives to take its place, so there is no close season of the type found in coarse or game fishing. Interestingly, today's sea angler no longer works on the 'chuck it and chance it' technique of yesteryear. Instead, the average sea angler is a specialist interested in one or two species of fish. For some it is flatfish, bass, wrasse or mullet, for others the speedy tope, thrashing conger or mighty shark. Modern tackle and techniques combined with an in-depth knowledge of baits and habitats means that in many cases sea anglers today catch only the species they have set out to catch. Their knowledge is gained from both personal experiences and the writings of other successful anglers, and today's magazine shelves are filled with specialist sea angling publications all loaded with advice and good, sound knowledge.

Sea angling is on the increase. Each season thousands of new anglers enter the sea-fishing world. Some come as match anglers, some to swell the ranks of sea angling clubs, while some come to fish on their own. Whether to catch mackerel or monster fish is up to the individual; the main thing is to enjoy the sport, its companionship and its pitfalls.

1 *Sea Tackle*

Once there was a theory that any gear could be used for sea fishing. Fortunately today's sea angler realizes that this is the wrong approach. Specialist sea angling is now very popular and any good tackle shop carries a reliable and basic range of sea tackle. The trick is for the angler to assess his local fishing, and by watching and asking the more experienced local anglers, to choose tackle that is right for the job in hand. To rush into any shop and buy on the spur of the moment is the wrong approach. An outfit that looks great in the shop window may prove useless in the locality you intend to fish. Remember also that salt water will soon find any flaws in the tackle you buy. To avoid a rusting mess on your hands make sure that rings, reel seats and exposed metal parts are of the finest quality. Cheap tackle is just that and is not good enough for use in salt water.

SHORE TACKLE

Choosing the right rod and reel for shore fishing is critical and depends greatly on the area you intend to fish and the species you hope to catch.

Rods

Beach casters normally come in a range of three casting weights. These are 2–4oz, 4–6oz and 6–8oz. Of the three, the 4–6oz caster is the most versatile. However, it may be too heavy or too light for some areas. This is where it pays to seek the advice of tackle dealers and anglers with experience of the beaches you are most likely to visit. Once you have decided on a weight of rod you must then consider length. The solution to this is to handle various patterns until you find one that feels right in your hand.

When light fishing for mullet or spinning for flounder or bass, a freshwater float rod or a carp rod are ideal. Remember, however, that the fittings on such a rod are not constructed to withstand salt water corrosion.

Reels

Reels are also important, and fortunately there is now a wide range of multiplying and high-quality fixed-spool reels designed specifically for shore fishing. There was a time when fixed spools were rather frowned upon, however, today's models and designs are well up to standard, allowing long-distance casting without the ever-present fear of your line turning into a savage bird's nest. Shimano probably produce the best range of both multiplying and fixed-spool sea reels in the United Kingdom.

BOAT TACKLE

Rods

For general boatwork a 30lb class boat rod is the norm, and as its rating implies, such a rod is designed for use with 30lb BS line. For heavier work in strong tides a 50lb class rod may be essential, and if big conger shark or giant skate are the quarry then an 80lb class rod may be called for. Always choose a rod which has a tip roller or tip and butt roller rings. You may have to use a wire line and without a roller or two you will quickly destroy this costly piece of tackle.

Up-Tide Rods

Up-tide rods are designed to cast the lead up and away from the boat. Normally these rods come in two unequal sections. Basically designed for light line fishing, they are 9–10ft long in total. There are many well-designed up-tide rods available, but before purchasing such a rod you must decide whether or not you will use it regularly – not all areas are suitable for up-tide fishing.

Reels

For all aspects of boat fishing the Shimano range offers the finest quality at good prices. For general boat work the TLD 20 or TLD 25 models are perfect as both incorporate a lever drag system which is superior to any other reel available in the United Kingdom. For the up-tide work the Shimano Triton Speedmaster, the Abu 6000 or the Daiwa Millionaire are all reliable reels with lots of big fish to their credit.

Lines

Nylon monofilament is the most popular line on sale in the world and every tackle shop stocks a dozen brand names. For beach and boat fishing it is better to purchase bulk spools as this allows line replacement at lower costs. Remember, however, that all nylon should be stored out of sunlight. Replace all lines on a regular basis and never attempt to use the same line for several seasons as all nylon will break down with use. If you leave a line on for too long it may cost you a good fish.

Wire Lines

For boat fishing in exceptionally strong tides a wire line can be an asset. The wire cuts through the tide flow and allows the use of lighter leads. Wire comes in single-strand and braided versions; the single strand is the most reliable.

Hooks

Anglers often spend a lot of money on a rod and reel, and then cut costs by trying to use cheap hooks. Remember that it is the hook that attaches you to the fish, so do not economize but buy the best. A good, heavy-duty hook for general boat work is the Mustad or Diawa O'Shaugnessey pattern. For lighter beach or smaller fish work an Aberdeen style hook is excellent. Carry a range of hook sizes plus a sharpening stone and you will not go wrong.

Swivels

As with hooks, there are many types of swivel and again, there are many cheap patterns which should be avoided like the plague. The best patterns available in the United Kingdom are the Berkley range (from the United States) – these are totally reliable.

Feathers and Lures

Mackerel feathers made out of modern synthetics are good for catching fish and should become a standard item for any boat angler's kit. Artificial eels and fish are a vital part of the wreck angler's armoury, and these are available in a wide range of colours and sizes. When going on a wreck outing at least twenty artificial baits should be carried.

Muppets

Plastic squid in various colours and sizes are effective deep-water baits and available from all good tackle shops.

Pirks

Heavy chromed or coloured lead-filled jigs useful for cod fishing in deep water, pirks are the sort of bait many anglers make at home. Sections of chrome piping filled with lead make a perfect substitute for expensive commercially made pirks.

Sliding Links

Lead links are essential for boat fishing with ledger tackle. The best patterns are the zip slider and the ashpole boom, and for deep-water work the Eddystone long boom is good.

A magnificent 32-pound cod. Fish of this size require the best of tackle.

2 Bass

The bass is an unmistakable fish which is handsome and rakish with a large spiky dorsal fin and heavy, silver body scales. The backs of young bass vary in colour from bluish-grey to greenish-grey, while mature specimens have dusky-grey backs and tarnished-silver sides. In prime condition the bass has a heavy and muscular look, with a hard and rather bony head and a huge mouth. Obviously a fast-moving predator, the bass is well suited to a life of hunting in heavy seas and along rugged rock gullies. Most rod-caught bass weigh 2–6lb and a fish of over 12lb is classed as a magnificent specimen. They can, however, reach weights of well over 20lb.

As bass are not prolific and are extremely slow growing, stocks have been savagely decimated by both anglers and commercial fishing interests. Continental buyers pay inflated prices for bass, and this in turn has led to the bass being exploited to a point where they are now something of an endangered species. For this reason many anglers and charter boat skippers now fish to preset bag limits. Once this limit is reached fishing either ceases or additional fish are played out and released.

In the British Isles bass can be caught from the Suffolk coast round to the Welsh coast, and while occasional fish may be taken north of these areas, such catches are rare. Bass are also common off the south and west coasts of Ireland. The species shows a liking for fresh water and many estuaries are noted for the quality of their bass fishing – West Country estuaries such as the Dart, Teign, Exe, Fowey and Fal, for example, are typical of the sort of estuary that attracts bass.

Bass.

Basically, however, bass are a rough water species that thrive in areas subjected to tidal rips, overfalls and generally heavy seas. In Ireland long, open storm beaches are perfect for bass fishing. These beaches fish best after an onshore gale. The pounding seas churn up the sand, releasing crabs, sand eels and other food to the ever-waiting bass. Harbours and piers also hold an attraction for extra large bass. These big and usually solitary fish become scavengers happy to glean a good living from the bait fish or fish entrails that are jettisoned by commercial fishing boats. Although bass can be caught

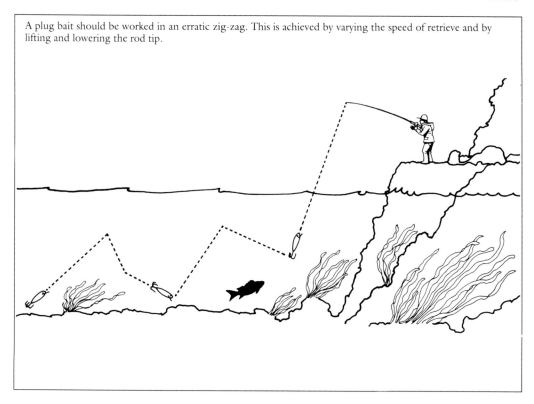

A plug bait should be worked in an erratic zig-zag. This is achieved by varying the speed of retrieve and by lifting and lowering the rod tip.

Fig 1   A jerky retrieve for bass.

at any time of the year the effective bass season lasts from April to October, with May, June and September as the top bass fishing months.

SHORE FISHING METHODS

Spinning

For the angler who likes to cover a lot of ground, spinning is a pleasant technique to use for bass fishing. Armed only with a light rod, reel and haversack to carry tackle and refreshments, the spin fisherman is free to wander the shoreline casting into each likely area. Bass of all sizes respond to artificial baits although few anglers spin fish on a

regular basis. Rocky coastlines offer the best potential for this style of angling.

Artificial baits are legion and it is easy to overspend in any tackle shop; instead it is better to fish a limited selection of carefully selected lures. Toby spoons from Sweden make a good basis on which to start. These elongated spoons come in a variety of lengths and weights and can be guaranteed to catch bass when those fish come within casting range. The more expensive Abu plug baits (from Sweden) can also be a top fish catcher. Plugs come in a range of shapes (see Fig 8) and in three basic types: floaters, which are designed to work on the surface; fast sinkers, which sink rapidly; and slow sinkers, which drop slowly through the water. Spinners are simply cast out and

Bass. One of the hardest fighting fish on the British list.

Sunset bass angler in southern Ireland. Inch beach is a typical storm beach, at its best soon after a gale.

A bass taken on live sandeel in the Channel Islands. Sandeel used live or dead is one of
the best all-round bass baits.

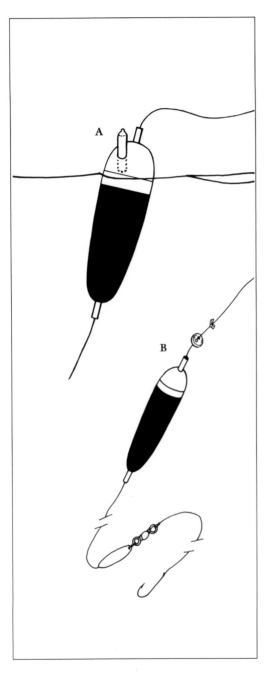

retrieved at varying speeds, but plugs need a little more thought. The object of any artificial lure is to imitate a natural fish, and while the spinner represents a fish in perfect condition, the plug is designed to look like a damaged bait which is easy for the bass to catch. To get the best action out of a plug it should be retrieved in a jerky manner by increasing or decreasing the rate of retrieve (see Fig 1).

Float Fishing

Generally carried out from rocks or harbour walls, float fishing is a pleasant and rewarding way of catching fish. For this style of angling a sliding float should be used (see Fig 2). Remember to keep the float on the small size as although big, bulky floats may look good, they can thoroughly frighten a taking fish. The float should be set roughly to the mid-water mark (see Fig 3) and the bait used could be a fish cutting, a live prawn (see Fig 5), or a lip-hooked sandeel or small, live fish (see Fig 4).

Bottom Fishing

Most shore-caught bass fall to standard bottom tackle. The best tackle to use is a simple one-hook paternoster rig (see Fig 6). Although bass of all sizes will fall to worm or shellfish baits, the better quality bass definitely succumb to the 'big bait, big fish' theory. Half a mackerel, a whole calamari squid or a large chunk of cuttlefish flesh are ideal to use as bait. The bait should be cast out to land on sand patches which are surrounded by rough ground on the sea bed. On open sand or shingle beaches the bait should be cast so that it falls into any known gully down which bass may venture in search of food. This style of bass fishing is a waiting game where blanks are the norm

Fig 2 'A' is a night float and 'B' a sliding float.

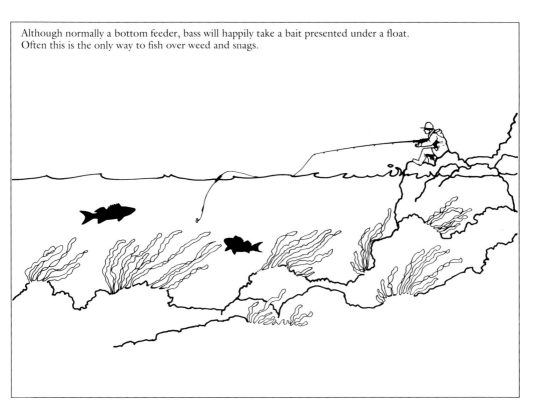

Although normally a bottom feeder, bass will happily take a bait presented under a float. Often this is the only way to fish over weed and snags.

Fig 3   The float must be set to clear upthrust weeds on the rocks.

and successes are few. Big baits should be presented on size 4-0 or 6-0 pre-sharpened hooks – far too many good bass have escaped when a small hook has snapped or bent out of shape.

BOAT FISHING METHODS

Artificial lures work as well from a boat as from the shore. In shallow waters these baits can be cast in the conventional manner, but in deeper water trolling is the best way to present an artificial lure.

Trolling

Trolling entails dragging a spinner, plug or, better still, a rubber sandeel behind a moving boat. To keep the bait working well below the surface a substantial weight must be used, and depending on the strength of the tide this lead should weigh 6–12oz. The best lead to use for this sort of fishing is a banana-shaped trolling lead (see Fig 7). This style of lead has a swivel at one end and a simple wire loop at the other. The reel line should be tied directly to this swivel. The trace should be made up with a sturdy link swivel which is clipped directly to the wire lead loop. The trace length should be

17

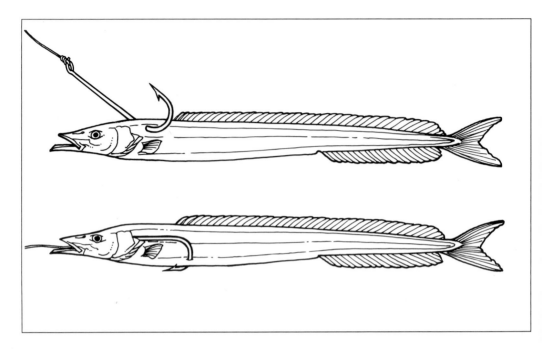

Fig 4   Sandeels are best used alive. This shows the two best methods of hooking live eels.

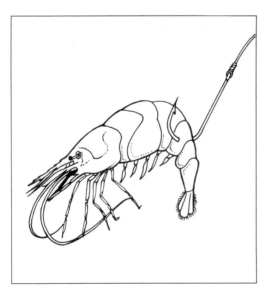

Fig 5   Live prawns should be hooked just once through a tail section. This keeps them lively and attractive to fish.

6–10ft. Bites are generally solid affairs and the fish normally hooks itself.

Bottom Fishing from an Anchored Boat

In recent years bottom fishing with the boat anchored on a known hot spot has produced some remarkably large bass. Basically a simple technique using a standard running ledger rig and long trace, the secret of this style of angling lies in the type and quality of the bait being used. Big bass are normally predatory creatures which expect mainly to catch their food alive and very definitely fresh. Top bait to use is whole calamari squid or long strips of fresh cuttlefish (see Fig 9), while live mackerel or half of a fresh mackerel also work well.

Boat-caught bass will normally pick up a bait and run with it held in their lips. Only when the fish is satisfied that there is no

Rocks provide the shore angler with a good position from which to cast into deep water.

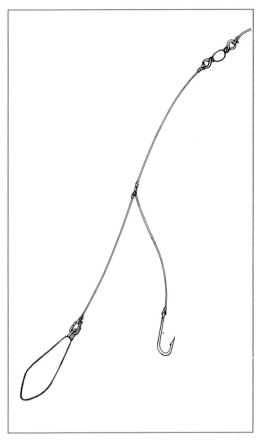

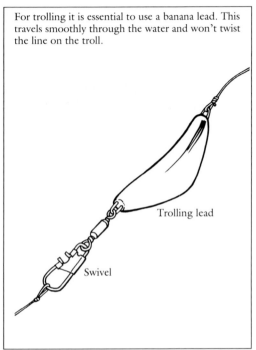

For trolling it is essential to use a banana lead. This travels smoothly through the water and won't twist the line on the troll.

Trolling lead

Swivel

Fig 7   Banana-shaped trolling lead.

Fig 6   Simple one-hook paternoster.

danger will the fish start to swallow the bait properly, and for this reason it pays the angler to hold the rod with the reel in free spool. When a bite does occur the fish can take the line freely yet will still be under the control of the angler.

Drift-Lining

This is a long-established way of catching bass which works best in estuaries and large harbours. Drift-line fishing is essentially a light tackle technique where the bait is fished without a weight when possible, and

with the minimum amount of lead to hold the bait down in a strong tidal flow. The bait to use for this style of fishing is live sandeel. The whole object of this style of angling is to present the bait as naturally as possible. To do this the sandeel should be hooked once through the lower jaw or once under the skin at the back of its neck – both hooking techniques will allow the bait to swim naturally. Once the boat is anchored in the tidal flow the bait should be dropped gently into the water and allowed to swim off freely with the prevailing tidal run. Bass working up the tide will then see and intercept the eel as a natural food item. Live sand eels should be kept in a well-aerated livebait tank – dead eels can be used but they are less attractive to a bass than the free-swimming eel.

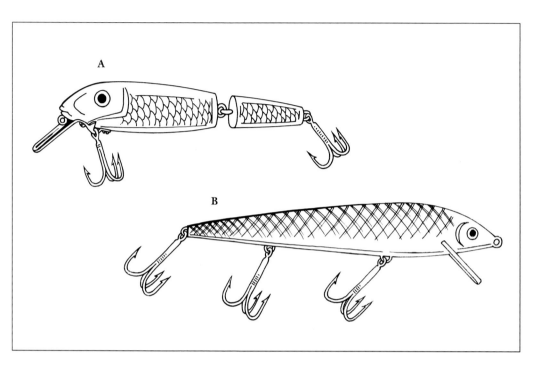

Fig 8 · Plug types: 'A' is a jointed plug; 'B' is a Rapala lure.

A chunk of cuttle fish can be made more attractive by frilling out the end of the bait to imitate moving tentacles.

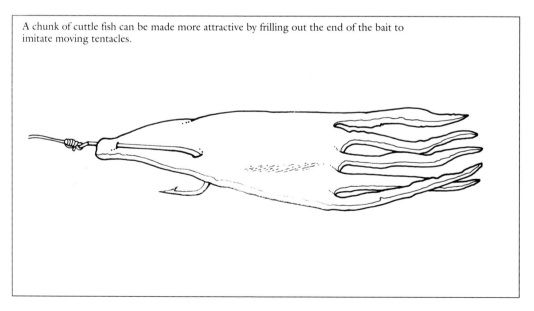

Fig 9   Cuttlefish bait for bass.

3 Cod and Ling

Cod have a widespread distribution, being found seasonally off every section of the British and Irish coastlines. In the southern half of the United Kingdom they are very much a winter fish, while in northern waters they are resident throughout the year. Cod can be caught both from the shore and from boats and their availability makes them the most popular of British sea fish.

Southern cod are on average far larger than the fish caught in cold northern seas, but what the northern fish lack in size they more than make up for in quantity. Southern fish are nowhere near as prolific as the northern ones but they can grow to 50lb or more in weight. Southern cod of 20lb are commonly caught and most winter seasons produce the odd 40lb specimens. In

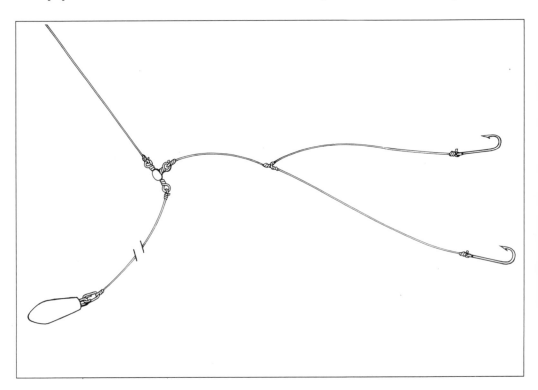

Fig 10 A two-hook paternoster.

Playing a big cod. Cod are powerful fish that should be 'pumped' carefully to the surface.

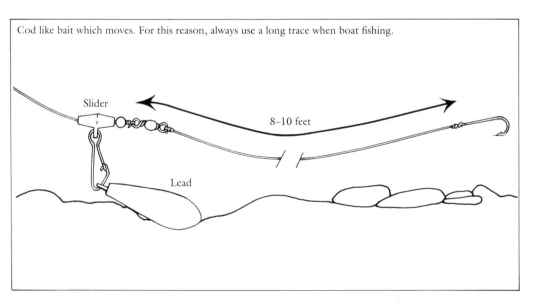

Cod like bait which moves. For this reason, always use a long trace when boat fishing.

Slider

8–10 feet

Lead

Fig 11 Typical trace for cod.

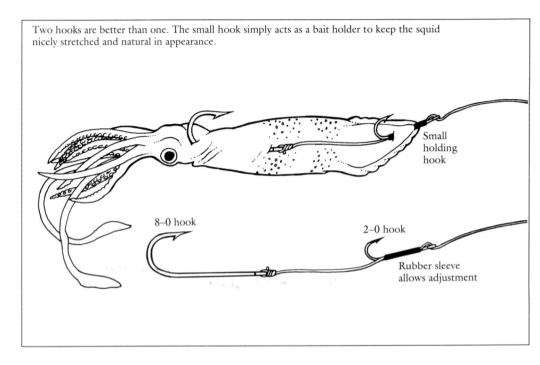

Two hooks are better than one. The small hook simply acts as a bait holder to keep the squid nicely stretched and natural in appearance.

Small holding hook

8–0 hook

2–0 hook

Rubber sleeve allows adjustment

Fig 12 Squid bait for cod.

northern waters a twenty pounder can be classed as a spectacular catch.

Most cod weighing 20lb and more are caught from boats while beach-caught fish tending to be much smaller. Occasionally, however, a lucky beach angler will set the hook into a monster fish. These very big fish normally occur off rock marks or steep beaches where deep water is within easy casting range. Normally a roving species, cod often take up permanent residence on deepwater wreck marks. They are bottom feeders and will eat just about anything edible that comes their way. Crabs, lobsters, worms, shellfish, fish and squid are all eaten when available, and cod will also suck up rubbish. I have seen fish with plastic cups, bottle tops, plastic, and bits of metal in their stomach linings – proof that the cod packs

hoover the sea bed like giant vacuum cleaners.

The cod is not an attractive fish, with a huge head, pot belly and sharply tapering body. Despite its odd shape a big cod fresh from the sea has an attraction all of its own although they are not good fighting fish and rarely show much spirit when hooked. A prolific spawner, the cod sheds eggs by the million but few survive to maturity and many, in fact, fall victim to their own kind.

Cod are a bottom dwelling and feeding species which means that for both shore and most boat fishing the bait must be presented on or close to the sea bed. The only real exception to this rule is when you are cod fishing over a wreck. Wreck cod will often feed and swim 20–30ft above the main bulk of a wreck.

SHORE FISHING METHODS

Most beach anglers use a single- or double-hook paternoster rig for cod fishing (see Fig 10). Cod have large mouths and an appetite to match, and for this reason big baits on size 4-0 hooks should be used. The bait used varies from area to area: from the Kent coast and up the east coast lugworm is the best bait; further north mussels and cockles seem to produce the most fish; and further south a lugworm tipped with a squid strip is an excellent fish catcher. Inshore cod are bold biters and drag the rod tip hard round when they take a bait, so the majority of shore-caught cod are taken in shows of

strength. Spending a whole night on a winter cod beach can be a chilling experience and therefore warm clothing, food and hot drinks are as essential as good fishing tackle.

BOAT FISHING METHODS

Using Natural Baits

Big cod and strong tides often go hand in hand, and for this reason the boat angler's tackle should be kept as simple as possible. A plain running ledger incorporating a sliding lead boom is the best terminal rig for the job. Cod like a bait that moves freely with the movement of the tide, so an 8–10ft trace should be used (see Fig 11). This allows the bait to flutter enticingly over the sea bed.

As mentioned above, cod baits vary from one locality to another. Where big cod exist the best all-round bait is calamari squid. These small squid are imported in 5lb boxes which are kept deep frozen until required. Never thaw out squid in fresh water, but instead allow it to thaw out naturally on the way to the fishing grounds. Squid should be used whole (see Fig 12) and when big cod are expected two squid mounted in a 'T' shape should be employed (see Fig 13). Cod hunt a great deal by smell and the squid bait should therefore be changed every twenty minutes – if left longer the scent will be washed out of the bait. Alternatively whole small fish and fillets of fish can be used as cod baits. Freshly caught pouting make excellent cod bait and can be used alive or dead, or as a cut bit.

Attractor Spoon Fishing

Cod are active hunters finding food by sight, scent and vibration. To help these fish

This method has produced many monster cod for southern anglers. The theory is that the tide pushing against the T-section makes the bait lift and waver off the bottom.

Double squid

Fig 13 'T' method of hooking a double squid.

A 28lb cod caught off the Isle of Wight. The Isle of Wight is Britain's big cod hot spot. Most winter seasons it produces fish of forty or more pounds.

An 18lb ling. Very much a pack fish, ling are common over deepwater wrecks.

locate the bait many anglers use a plastic or metal attractor spoon set 12–15in uptrace of the hook and bait (see Fig 14). The attractor spoon blade is designed to revolve at speed in the tidal flow, and this movement sets up a pulsating vibration which big cod often find irresistible.

Many anglers lose cod by striking before the bite has had time to develop. To avoid such losses the rod should be held at all times. When the first 'pull' occurs the angler should release a yard of line as this will allow the fish to mouth at the bait without feeling any major resistance. Often this process will have to be repeated several times before the cod begins to swallow the bait. Once the angler is confident that the fish has taken well, line should slowly be retrieved until the whole weight of the fish is felt. At this stage

the angler should lift solidly into the fish rather than strike sharply. Provided the hook is sharp it should set easily into the fish. Size 6-0 or 8-0 hooks of the O'Shaugnessy type are best for this type of cod fishing.

Pirk Fishing for Cod

Over sunken wrecks or submerged reefs pirk fishing can be a deadly way of catching cod. A pirk is simply a chromed section of lead-filled metal tied directly to the reel line. At the lower section of a pirk bait a wire loop and a heavy split ring are attached to take the hook. Shop-bought pirks normally come equipped with a huge, dangling treble hook (see Fig 15). Hooks of this kind should not be used as they tend to act as a grapnel catching up in rocks and wreckage, and they

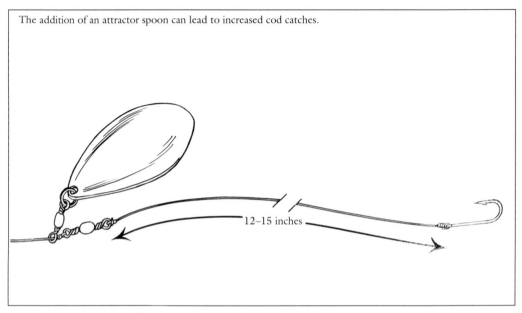

The addition of an attractor spoon can lead to increased cod catches.

12–15 inches

Fig 14 Attractor spoon for cod.

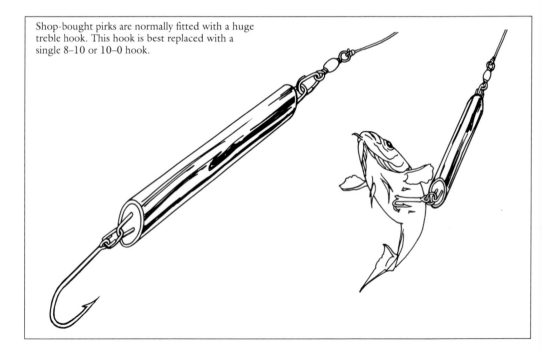

Shop-bought pirks are normally fitted with a huge treble hook. This hook is best replaced with a single 8–10 or 10–0 hook.

Fig 15 Pirks for cod.

foul-hook fish on a regular basis – in northern waters they are called 'murderers'. In situations where fish are shoaled up, the treble usually ends up everywhere but in the cod's mouth, so most anglers replace the treble with a large single hook (see Fig 16).

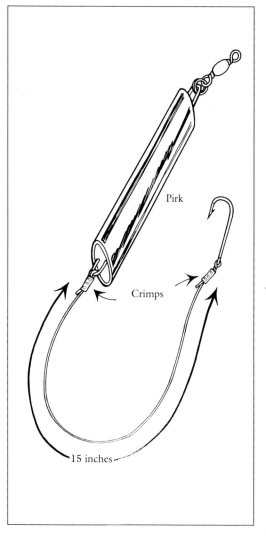

Fig 16 Pirks work well when used with a 15-inches trace and natural bait.

This simple operation takes only seconds and cuts tackle loss and the percentage of foul-hooked fish to an acceptable minimum.

A pirk is designed to simulate a bait-sized fish and to give the lure movement it is worked by lifting and lowering the rod tip. Presumably the hunting cod see the lure as a damaged fish darting upwards before dropping with an attractive, fluttering motion. Pirks now come in a dazzling range of shapes and colours, some being very expensive items of equipment. To cut costs many anglers make their own lures from various lengths of lead-filled chrome piping – old office chairs or pram handles are typical sources of material.

Baited Pirks

On days when the cod are being finicky or when large ling are mixed in with the shoaling cod, a baited pirk can be a deadly way of going about catching them. For this style of fishing the single hook should be attached to the pirk by a 6–9in length of 150lb BS long-liner nylon. Both the baits and pirk should be worked by raising and lowering the rod tip.

Bites on baited pirk are normally very solid affairs. Once hooked the fish should be hustled up and away from the wreck or other obstructions – if you give the fish a chance to get its head down, the chances are that you will lose both the fish and your terminal tackle. Ling are extremely fond of baited pirks.

Cod Feathers or Muppets

Where cod are thickly shoaled, a set of two or three feathers or a plastic squid (muppets) can be an excellent way of catching them. These artificials are normally fished above a lead or hookless pirk (see Fig 17).

A ling caught on a baited pirk.

A winter cod angler. With the exception of Scotland, which has cod on a year-round basis, the cod is very much a winter species.

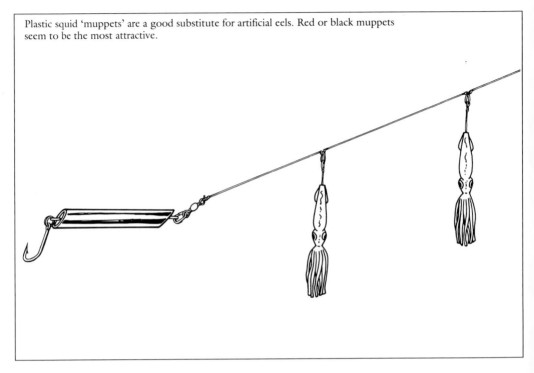

Plastic squid 'muppets' are a good substitute for artificial eels. Red or black muppets seem to be the most attractive.

Fig 17 A pirk and two muppets on droppers.

LING

Although ling have elongated eel-like bodies they are true members of the cod family. Despite this elongated body, the double dorsal fins and the broad head, tooth-filled jaws and single long chin barbule make the ling an easy species to identify. Ling vary in colour from one location to another but are normally greenish-grey or greyish-brown. The basic body colour is overlaid with darker spots and blotches, these markings being more noticeable on the smaller specimens. Very much a deep-water species, ling are most common around deep, sunk reefs and wrecks. They shoal well above a wreck mark and are adept at intercepting baits on the way down. Ling are normally caught on baited pirks of the type used by cod anglers.

4 *Black and Red Bream*

The black and red bream are handsome fish although neither grow to a large size, a five-pounder being a large specimen for either species. However, what these fish lack in weight they more than make up for in fighting ability. Both species are limited in distribution and both are also basically deep-water dwellers. Most of these inshore fish are taken from rock marks in the Channel Islands.

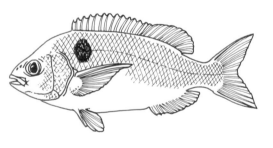

Red bream.

The red bream is orange-red in colour with silvery-pink sides. This distinctive coloration along with its dark shoulder patch makes the red bream an easy fish to identify. The eyes of the red bream are very large which is sure sign that it is a deep-water species. While the average rod-caught red bream weighs 12½lb, individual specimens to nearly 8lb in weight have been recorded, although fish of this calibre are rare. Red bream are often common on deep-water wreck marks and such fish live in perpetual darkness, feeding at any time of the night or day. In shallower areas red bream are very definitely nocturnal feeders. Small red bream seem to feed on shellfish while the larger fish will take fish, squid or worm baits. Red bream are strong fish but they do not compare in strength to the black bream. Black bream are much sought after by boat-anglers but very occasionally they can be caught from the shore. Similar in shape to the red bream, the black bream is a dusky-silver fish often sporting distinctive dark, vertical side stripes. Black bream seldom attain a weight in excess of 5½lb. Both species are confined to marks off the south and south-west coastlines of Britain but black bream are tightly distributed on marks off the Sussex, Hampshire, Dorset and Cornish coastlines. Littlehampton in Sussex was once 'queen' of the black bream harbours with charter boats operating from this port fishing the famed Kingmere Rocks. Unfortunately, anglers have been responsible for a serious overkill as far as bream are concerned. Nowadays charter skippers and thinking anglers restrict their catches in a drive to conserve bream stocks. A decade ago it seemed that black bream were hovering on the verge of extinction but fortunately sensible angling policies have reversed this trend and black

Black bream are always a popular species, particularly with light tackle enthusiasts.

Very much a deepwater species, red bream like sunken reefs or wrecks.

Although black bream are not as numerous as they once were, there are still enough to ensure good fishing.

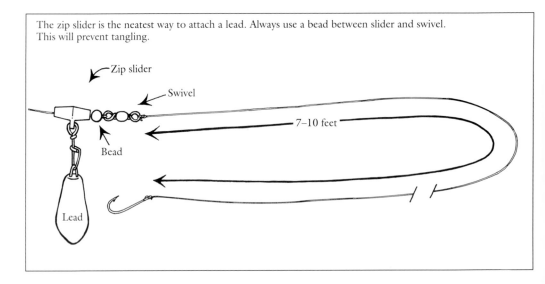

The zip slider is the neatest way to attach a lead. Always use a bead between slider and swivel. This will prevent tangling.

Fig 18   Long trace for bream.

bream seem to be making a welcome come-back.

FISHING METHODS

Black bream feed and shoal at varying levels linked to the rise and fall of the prevailing tidal flow. At slack water they normally confine their feeding activities to the sea bed. Later, as the tide starts to run, they may rise well up towards the surface. Red bream tend to stay on the sea bed during daylight hours, only rising as the light fades – this applies only to red bream living and feeding in waters where light can penetrate to the bottom.

For both species a standard running ledger is the most effective terminal rig to use. When black bream are your target species a long, flowing trace should be used – as a rough guide, this should be as long as your rod (see Fig 18). Lead weights should

be kept as small as tidal flows will allow. Bream fishing calls for lighter lines than normal sea angling, and the use of these light lines means that lighter weights (½–¾oz) are often sufficient. Obviously the amount of lead used on any given mark is dictated by the tidal run on any given day – for example, spring tides will call for more lead than neap tides. Even in the worst of tidal conditions most English bream can be fished with a maximum of 3oz of lead. The exception to the use of light lines is deep-water wreck marks where they cannot be used.

The lead should run freely on the reel line. A zip slider should be used to attach the lead to the line, but when the fish are finicky on the bottom so that rough snagging is likely, the lead weight can be fished on a nylon dropper (see Fig 19). To cut losses to a minimum the lead can be attached by a rubber band or garden tie – under pressure either will part, thus

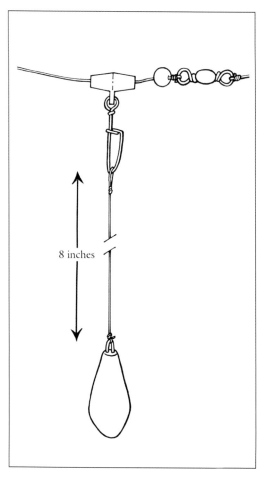

Fig 19   Nylon lead dropper.

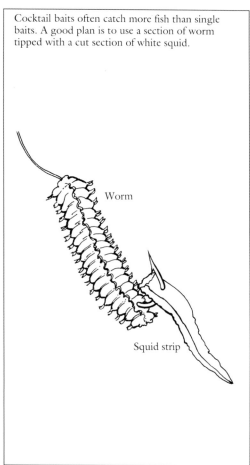

Cocktail baits often catch more fish than single baits. A good plan is to use a section of worm tipped with a cut section of white squid.

Worm

Squid strip

Fig 20   Cocktail bait for black bream.

8 inches

releasing the bulk of the tackle. Leads are expendable but valuable fishing time can be lost if an entirely new set of terminal gear has to made up.

For red bream a static bait seems to catch well while black bream respond more readily to a bait that moves slowly over the sea bed. The most deadly black bream method is to trot the bait over the sea bed and then retrieve it slowly so that the bait comes up to the surface. With this method bites can occur anywhere between the bottom and mid-water level. Both bream are bold biters, but the black bream is a definite nibbler. Many anglers strike at the first rattle of the rod top – this is incorrect. Ignore the first tweaks and allow the bite to develop. Once a black bream gains confidence it will take the bait firmly and this is the time to strike. For black bream a combination or cocktail

A combination of nightfall and a rising tide often produce good fishing.

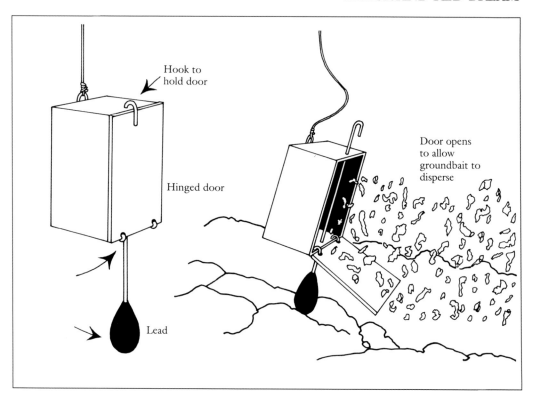

Hook to
hold door

Hinged door

Door opens
to allow
groundbait to
disperse

Lead

Fig 21   Bait dropper.

bait can be deadly, a typical combination consisting of a squid strip and a ragworm or lugworm (see Fig 20). Red bream prefer fish or squid used on its own.

Paternoster Tackle

All bream like a bait that moves and a simple wire or paternoster rig used with a long trace can be deadly. This sort of rig works best when the tide starts to slacken; at full slack the trace length should be shortened and the boom moved up the line. Hooks should be on the small size – a size 1 or 2 freshwater scale should be used for all forms of bream fishing.

Groundbait

Being a shoal fish, bream respond well to groundbait – chopped squid and chopped worm are the best ingredients. Many anglers use a special bait dropper (see Fig 21) to get the bait down to the level of the sea bed, but bait droppers of this kind have to be made up at home.

5 Conger

For many sea anglers the conger may be the largest sea fish they are likely to encounter. The rod-caught boat record stands at over 100lb and eels far larger than this have been recorded by commercial fishermen. Catching huge conger is not just for boat anglers as many large eels can be found close to the shore. It is unlikely that such fish reach the massive weights of their deep-water cousins, but even so fish over 70lb have been caught by harbour anglers. Probably every major harbour in Britain has its monster conger legend. Most of these fish stories are little more than a figment of someone's fertile imagination, but some stories do contain a grain of truth.

Braye Harbour on Alderney in the Channel Islands holds some huge eels and some West Country harbours are also capable of producing hefty eels. Rock marks like Portland Bill in Dorset have been known to throw up the odd large conger. A shore-caught eel over 40lb in weight can be classed as a good specimen. Conger over 60lb are rare from rock or harbour marks, possibly because few anglers fish for them on a regular basis.

Boat anglers regularly hook up huge eels and most of these monsters are hooked over deep-water wreck marks, although many are lost when the tackle fouls on some substantial section of the wreck. Despite these losses, wreck eels of over 80lb are boated each season, the majority of these catches being taken over Channel wrecks or wrecks situated in the western approaches. North of Devon on the Welsh coast large conger seem to be scarce – the big ones seem to grow and thrive in the warmer waters of the south and south-west half of the United Kingdom.

CONGER FEEDING HABITS

Inshore conger are essentially nocturnal feeders which seldom begin to move until well after dark. The interesting thing is that these inshore eels will feed well from full dark until midnight, then go off the feed until about an hour before dawn. This pre-dawn feeding spell can be quite intense and may well produce a big catch of eels of mixed sizes.

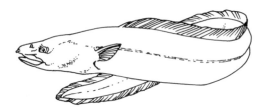

Conger.

Very much a summer and late autumn fish, inshore conger feed best on overcast nights. During October and early November inshore stocks are often topped up by the arrival of a few heavyweight offshore conger. Why these big eels move in at the beginning of winter has yet to be explained. The most popular theory is that it is a food foray – a brief raid on the rich inshore waters to mop up enough small fish to sustain them through the colder months ahead. Interestingly, winter boat anglers catch the occasional big conger while cod fishing. These outsize eels are normally caught over open bottom stretches virtually devoid of rocks or other obstructions. It seems likely that these big, open-ground eels are fish which have moved in to stock up on the onshore feeding grounds and are now on their way back out to the deeps where they will spend the winter.

The fact that conger are nocturnal feeders means little in deep water. Below 30 fathoms it is unlikely that the fish are even aware of light. Their whole world is dominated by constant darkness. For this reason the feeding cycle of deep-water conger may be dictated by tidal flow rather than light penetration. Even then, I suspect that conger could be taken at any stage of the tide if it were possible for the angler to fish through the tidal flow. In most instances the offshore wrecks can mostly be fished at anchor only during the slack water period, which is why slack water is traditionally reckoned to be the best time to catch congers.

Food and Related Bait

By nature conger are natural predators and much of their lives is spent in active pursuit of live food including fish, crustaceans, such as crab and lobster, and cephalopods, such

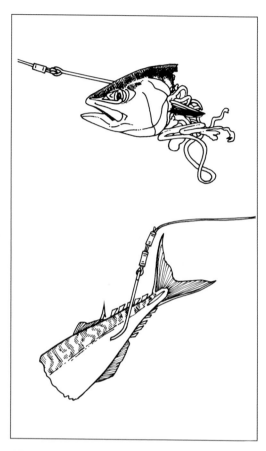

Fig 22 The head and guts or tail of a mackerel makes excellent bait for conger.

as squid, cuttlefish and octopus. Conger will also deign to scavenge, picking up fresh dead and damaged food items. There is a popular belief that conger will eat just about anything that comes their way. However, this is just an old wives' tale that is widely repeated but which has little basis in fact. Harbour conger used to the constant dumping of waste bait fish may be less choosey than the average eel, but even these fish will take a small fresh bait in preference to a large stale one.

Such positions on rocks can be dangerous. Always watch out for that extra-big wave.

Three fine conger, the best being 58lb, taken from an area of rough ground.

Fig 23 A top conger bait is the head and guts of a mackerel. The best baits are produced by cutting three-quarters of the way through the fishbait, then pulling it apart by hand.

Conger are not fussy about the type of fish they catch and eat, and inshore conger will take wrasse, pouting, rockling, mackerel and so on, although offshore pouting may make up the bulk of the conger's food intake. Big conger will also eat small conger. Obviously, oily fish such as mackerel, horse mackerel, herring and pilchard are highly attractive to hunting conger. When slashed with a knife all these fish give off an oil slick which helps the conger to home in on the smell source.

Whole or cut pouting are probably the most consistently deadly conger bait, and second must come the head and trailing stomach of a fresh mackerel (see Fig 22). To get a perfect bait the fish should be cut down from the back of the head to a point three-quarters of the way through the body (see Fig 23). The head can then be pulled

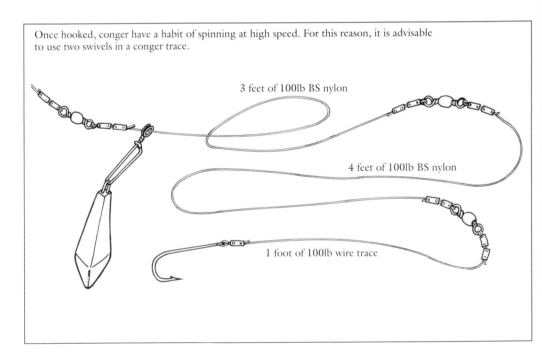

Once hooked, conger have a habit of spinning at high speed. For this reason, it is advisable to use two swivels in a conger trace.

3 feet of 100lb BS nylon

4 feet of 100lb BS nylon

1 foot of 100lb wire trace

Fig 24 Running ledger for conger.

away from the body leaving the guts attached. This bait should be hooked once through the eye sockets and although it may be messy it is a guaranteed fish catcher. The remainder of the body also makes a good bait, and again it should be hooked just once, but this time through the wrist of the tail. Too many anglers spoil their bait presentation by passing the hook repeatedly through the bait. This causes the bait to bunch and spoils its appearance.

TERMINAL TACKLE

Conger eels are strictly bottom feeders, hunting for their food amongst the rocks and wreckage in which they normally live. For both shore and boat fishing a basic running ledger (see Fig 24) is the only terminal tackle to use. Congers are not lead shy and long traces are not necessary – most serious conger anglers use a trace of 18–24in in length. Traditionally wire was always used for conger fishing and the trace

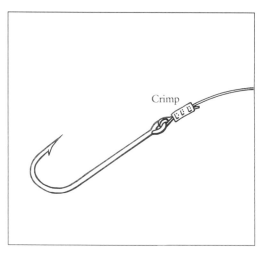

Fig 25   Crimping heavy nylon.

itself was normally made out of stiff stainless steel or brass wire. Outdated traces of this kind are still on sale, but they have no place in the modern angler's tackle box. Congers have ridges of tiny teeth in their mouths designed for gripping and crushing rather than cutting. For this reason traces can quickly and cheaply be made up from nylon-covered wire of 100lb BS or heavy-duty long-liner nylon.

Of the two materials the long-liner nylon makes the best trace as it is extremely tough yet still supple and easy to knot or crimp. The ideal BS nylon to use is 150lb BS. On wrecks where huge conger are known to exist this BS can be stepped up to 200lb. When using heavy nylon it should be knotted carefully (see Fig 25) leaving a long, free end which can be crimped once or even twice. To ensure strength the tail end of nylon should be tucked back into the crimp before the crimp itself is squeezed tight with a proper crimping tool (available from all tackle shops). The knot used is designed to tighten under pressure while crimps are a second insurance policy. Conger are strong and dogged fighters so make certain that only the best quality hooks and swivels are used for trace making. Anglers often spend a fortune on a rod, reel and line, and then scrimp on hooks and swivels. Remember the terminal tackle takes the violence meted out by a resisting eel – violence that will soon show up material defects. The best swivels are the Berkley barrel swivels and the best hooks are the O'Shaugnessey flat forged patterns in sizes 6-0 or 8-0 for shore fishing, and 8-0 or 10-0 for boat work.

CONGER BITES

The larger the conger the softer the bite. Why this should be no one can say, but it is

45

A typical wreck conger caught from a mid-channel mark.

Fishing close in off Alderney in the Channel Islands.

Big conger brought up from a deepwater wreck mark.

a fact. Small conger hit a bait like a runaway train but the big eels are more cautious. Premature striking loses a lot of fish and where conger are concerned it pays to give the biting eel ample time to get the bait well inside its mouth.

Fishing tip

Conger live in or around heavy obstructions where terminal tackle losses are inevitably high. To cut these losses to an acceptable minimum leads should be attached by heavy elastic bands or by strong garden ties. If a lead does slide into a crevice and jam, rod pressure will snap the rubber or wire linkage. The lead will be lost but the terminal rig and possibly a hooked eel will be saved.

PLAYING A CONGER

Conger are powerful fighters that have to be bullied from the word go. Allow a conger to wrap its tail around some solid object and it will pull itself quickly into a position where no amount of heaving will have any effect. The trick is to strike, heave and wind the reel handle as quickly as possible. If you are lucky these tactics will get the eel up and away from any obstructions. Once it is in open water maximum pressure can then be applied to drag it to the surface.

Watch out for a last minute crash dive when the fish sees the light or perhaps reaches the surface – many a monster conger has been brought within gaffing range and then turned the tables on the unfortunate angler with a sudden and unstoppable downward run for freedom.

6 Haddock, Whiting and Pouting

The three fish discussed in this chapter are all small members of the cod family. Of the three species haddock grows to the largest size, reaching a maximum weight of a little over 10lb. Haddock of this size are rare, most rod-caught specimens weighing less than 3lb. All three species can be caught from both boat and shore marks. All three are attractive fish, the haddock and whiting especially being very good to eat. The plump pouting, however, is a tasteless fish only useful as bait for catching other species.

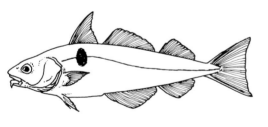

Haddock.

HADDOCK

This fish once had a widespread distribution, being particularly common off the coast of west Scotland and Northern Ireland. Individual pockets of very big fish were also found off the south coast of Cornwall. Unfortunately, high prices have meant that the once prolific haddock shoals have been decimated by commercial fishing fleets.

Closely related to cod, haddock are similar in many ways although they can easily be identified by their slightly forked tails, black lateral lines and dark shoulder spots on each side of their bodies. Haddock are true bottom feeders which live mainly on marine worms, crustacea, molluscs and small starfish. Large haddock will also catch and eat small fish of many kinds.

WHITING

If whiting reached the size of big cod they would be wonderful fish to catch on rod and line as their streamlined heads and bodies give them a far greater turn of speed than the rather cumbersome cod. Unfortunately, the average whiting taken on a rod weighs in at 1–2lb, and any whiting over 4lb in weight can be classed as a good catch. A five-pounder is the fish of a lifetime.

Whiting have a wide distribution and can be caught almost anywhere around the British Isles. On the south coast these fish are most common during the colder winter

A typical average-sized winter whiting.

Tim Williams of Witney and a 5¼ lb whiting.

Pouting often save the day when better fish refuse to feed.

Baited feathers are good for whiting, haddock, pouting and the like. The combination of colour and smell is highly attractive.

Whiting like bright colours combined with natural bait. For this reason baited feathers make a quick and easy – yet deadly – whiting rig.

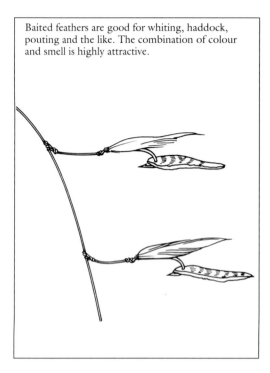

Fig 26 Feathers baited with mackerel strips.

months; further west they are an early summer species. Like the haddock the better specimens normally fall to boat anglers, but in food-rich areas small to average whiting can be caught by the after-dark shore angler. It is only necessary to look at the tooth-filled mouth of the whiting to see that this fish is an active predator which exists by preying on a multitude of small fish. Always popular as a table fish, the whiting is a popular species with all sea anglers.

Fig 27 Feathers baited for whiting.

POUTING

To the competition angler the easily caught pouting is a weight-building godsend, but to other anglers it is little more than a bait-robbing nuisance that attacks and ruins big baits intended for more sought-after species. In appearance the pouting is an attractive deep-bodied fish which is copper coloured, with or without dark vertical stripes depending on whether it lives on rocky or sandy ground. Although pouting give a sharp, rattling bite they put up little or no struggle once they have been hooked. Shore-caught pouting rarely weigh more than a few ounces while offshore fish can reach weights of 2–3lb. Freshly caught pouting make excellent bait for cod, bass, tope, conger and skate. They must, however, be used straight from the sea, as dead pouting decompose rapidly, so much so that many commercial fishermen call them 'stink alives'.

FISHING METHODS

Nothing special is required to catch any of these fish. The terminal rig for shore and boat fishing is a simple one-, two- or three- hook paternoster rig. Some boat anglers use three baited mackerel feathers (see Figs 26 and 27) and this can be a highly successful technique – presumably the bright feathers add to the attractiveness of the natural bait. A simple running ledger can also be used for boat fishing. This ledger rig is an excellent method to use when large whiting are on the move.

Baits

Worms, shellfish (for example, slipper limpets, mussels and cockles), squid strips and fish strips all catch fish. Beach anglers do better when using worms, while boat anglers make the best catches on the baits mentioned. Hook sizes 1-0 and 2-0 are ideal for all three species.

7 Flatfish

Good to eat and fun to catch, the various species of flatfish are popular with boat and shore anglers alike. The most widespread and most sought-after species is probably the flounder. Catching this and other flatfish is described on the following pages.

Brill and turbot: the prize catch of the boat angler.

Flounder fishing. Flounders are common during the winter months.

FLOUNDER

These fish have a widespread distribution range and can be found right around the coasts of Britain and Ireland. Flounder show a marked liking for fresh or brackish water, being most common in harbours, creeks and estuaries. Flounder can be caught throughout the year, but are most prevalent during the colder months. The flounder is a thick-bodied little fish with a large head and strong, tooth-filled jaws. Its back is normally greyish-brown, but this may vary from one locality to another; the underparts are normally white although occasionally a fish will be taken with a partially coloured underbody. Most flounder weigh around ¾lb, but they can reach a weight of 4lb. Active hunters, flounder feed on shrimps, worms, crabs and the occasional small fish.

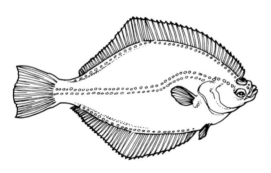

Flounder.

PLAICE

The plaice is one of the best known flatfish and is much sought after by anglers. Plaice grow to weights in excess of 8lb, but average rod-caught specimens weigh 1½–2lb. The back of a plaice is a rich brown colour overlaid with bold orange-red spots and the underside is white. Very much a spring and summer species, plaice are seldom caught during cold weather.

The other small flatfish are dab, sole, witch, megrim and topknot. Only the dab and the sole are of much interest to the angler, and both of these are normally taken while fishing for other species.

TURBOT

A turbot is very much a prize catch. Its large size, table quality and beautifully coloured back make it an angler's dream fish. Turbot are a fish of the tideswept offshore banks – the Varne at Dover, the Skerries off Dartmouth and the legendary Shambles bank off Weymouth. Turbot are fish of the summer months, and although the odd fish is caught during the winter or early spring, this is the exception rather than the rule.

Turbot are true predators with big mouths and sharp teeth which are ideally suited to catching and holding fish. Most big turbot hunt from ambush, normally picking a position just over the lip of a bank. From this spot they can intercept any small fish which is swept across the bank by the force of the tide. Not a shoal fish, the turbot may group to take advantage of a constant food stream. Turbot can reach a weight of 35lb although most rod-caught fish weigh up to 20lb.

BRILL

Large brill are often mistaken for small turbot. At face value both species are similar in outward appearances, however, a close examination will show that the body of the

A two-hook paternoster allows the flatfish angler to present two varied baits.

brill is more oval in shape than that of the turbot. The upper dorsal fin of a brill extends down over its eyes while the upper dorsal fin of the turbot is shorter.

Like turbot, brill vary in colour from one area to another, but generally the back colour is greyish-brown with a heavy freckling of dark spots and whitish patches and the underside is white. Like most flatfish both turbot and brill are taken with partially coloured underparts. Brill reach a maximum weight of 15lb but such fish are rare, the average size being 5–8lb. Like turbot, brill are most common off the south and south-west coastlines. They feed on small fish and prawns and like the turbot they are particularly fond of sand eels.

HALIBUT

This is the giant of the flatfish tribe, a fish of cold northern waters that can reach weights of up to 300lb. Never common, halibut are now extremely rare with most rod-caught fish being taken off the Orkney and Shetland Islands. Halibut are highly active predators that feed on a wide variety of

Fig 28   A flatfish paternoster.

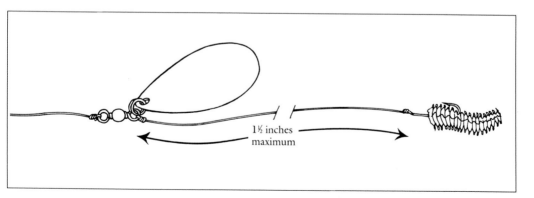

Fig 29   A baited spoon.

Both these brill were taken on live sandeel.

Plaice – plus attractor beads. The beads add interest to the natural bait.

bottom and mid-water fish. Easy to identify by its vast size, the halibut has an elongated diamond-shaped body with a greenish-brown back and white underside. Its mouth is huge and filled with sharp teeth. Solitary by nature, halibut are a hard species to catch on a rod and line, and often several seasons pass without a single fish being reported.

FISHING METHODS

Flounder and Plaice

Beach Fishing

For standard beach fishing a 2–4oz beach caster should be used. Both species are bottom feeders best caught on a one- or

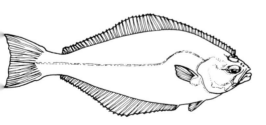

Halibut.

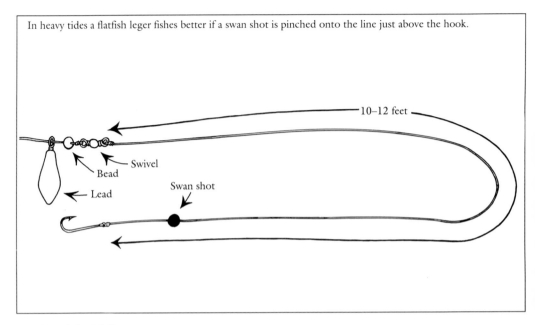

In heavy tides a flatfish leger fishes better if a swan shot is pinched onto the line just above the hook.

10–12 feet

Swivel

Bead

Lead

Swan shot

Fig 30   A flatfish leger.

two-hook nylon paternoster (see Fig 28). Lugworms, ragworms and soft or peeler crabs make the best baits. Plaice also show a liking for cocktail baits – for example, worm tipped with squid strip or soft crab.

Boat Fishing

Flounder tend to be an inshore species, often taken by the dinghy and small boat angler. Probably the most effective way of catching these fish is to use the baited spoon technique. Originally devised for flounder fishing in Langstone Harbour, the baited spoon rig (see Fig 29) is now used wherever flounder are common. Plastic spoons are generally better fish catchers than metal spoons, and to fish it properly the hook should be 1½in behind the spoon – longer hook lengths than this rarely catch fish. The idea is to create the illusion of a small

flounder making off with a large worm – larger flounders will then give chase and attempt to steal the worm. To be most effective the spoon should be retrieved slowly so that the lure and bait just skim the sea bed.

Plaice

Catching plaice from a drifting boat can be a pleasant and effective way of taking fish. A simple single-hook ledger rig should be used in conjunction with a long flowing trace (see Fig 30). The lead should be just heavy enough to hold the tackle down at the level of the sea bed, and to stop the bait from riding up I pinch a single SSG split shot on to the line a few inches from the baited hook. Both plaice and flounder have small mouths which call for narrow-gape, long-shanked size 1 or 2 shanked hooks.

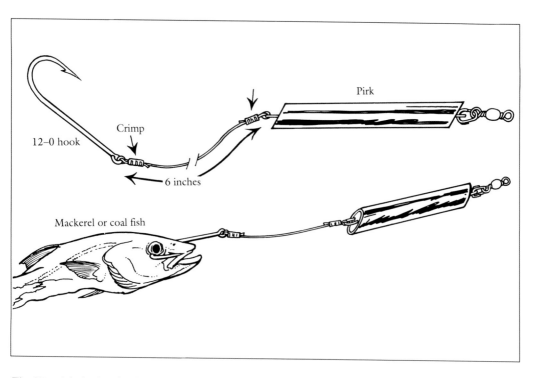

Fig 31   A baited pirk often catches better than an unbaited pirk.

Turbot and Brill

Although the odd small turbot can be taken from the beach, larger turbot and brill are very much fish of the tide-washed offshore banks. Both species like big baits and both have big mouths. Hooks of size 6-0 are ideal for use with fish fillet baits, and sizes 2-0 or 4-0 can be used with live or dead sand eels. Turbot traces should be made of 80lb nylon while for brill a slightly lighter trace can be used. Terminal tackle consists of a simple running ledger, again with a long flowing trace. Normally both species live in strong tides where heavy tackle is essential, hence the heavy trace material.

Halibut

By comparison, the mighty halibut makes all other flatfish look like midgets. Even a small specimen weighing 100lb is strong enough to require 80lb class tackle, and baits should also be on the large size. A top terminal rig is a heavy pirk fitted with a 12-0 Seamaster hook (see Fig 31). This pirk is then jigged by raising and lowering the rod tip. Basically a bottom feeder, halibut will follow a bait well up from the sea bed before hitting it, so a good technique is to lower the bait to the bottom, and then slowly jig and retrieve it up to the mid-water mark before lowering it and repeating the process.

Fish like these nice plaice are common on the Dartmouth skerries.

Chris Vince with a really fine Isle of Wight turbot.

8 Rays and Skates

There was a time when all skates and rays were classed as either thornback rays or common skates – if it was small it was a thornback and if it was big it was a common skate. Today's anglers, however, are record conscious and take the trouble to identify individual species correctly. Knowing what you have caught adds to the overall pleasure of angling and it may, if you are lucky, lead to your name appearing in the record books. For this reason I feel that it is advisable to list the most common species and their appearances here.

THORNBACK RAY

The thornback is probably the most common and the most widely sought after of British rays. As its name implies it is armed with a number of thorny spines on its back and tail. These can be sharp and it pays to carry a piece of old towelling with which to pick up these spiky fish. Thornbacks are variable in colour, usually brown or greyish-brown on their backs with this basic background colour overlaid with pale spots surrounded by borders of small dark spots. Smallish fish may have dark bands on their tail. The underparts are white. The average size is 7–12lb although fish over 20lb do occur.

Thornbacks have a wide distribution, being found right around the British Isles and southern Ireland. During the spring and summer months thornbacks move inshore to feed and during the winter they move well offshore. Thornbacks are bottom feeders which are happy to become scavengers when other food is in short supply. Catches indicate that thornbacks travel in small groups, each group consisting of one large female and a retinue of smaller males. Normally the female is caught first and the males follow in quick succession.

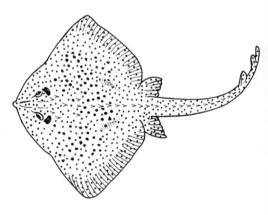

Blonde ray.

BLONDE RAY

While the thornback ray is a fish of semi-sheltered water, the blonde ray prefers to live and feed in hard tides. These rays are most common in the southern half of the

64

Channel from the Isle of Wight westward. Commonly reaching weights of 25–30lb, the blonde ray is a good fighter that can be relied upon to contest every yard of line gained. Blonde rays are less angular than the thornbacks and also lack the thorn-like spines. The back of this ray is sandy coloured with eight or more pale spots, and the whole of the fishes' back is heavily marked with small dark spots which extend to the wing margins. The underparts are white. Active hunters, blonde ray are normally taken on sand eel or strips of fresh mackerel.

HOMELYN OR SPOTTED RAY

This handsome ray is often confused with the blonde ray as both species have a similar basic appearance. The nose or snout of the spotted ray is more prominent than that of the blonde ray and the overall back colouring is darker. The pale spots on the back of the spotted ray are slightly less well defined than on the blonde ray, and each pale spot is bordered by a ring of small, dark spots. Essentially a shallow-water species, spotted rays are found all around the coastlines of the British Isles. Seldom reaching a weight of more than 5lb, spotted ray feed on worms, hermit crabs and small fish, although most rod-caught specimens are taken on fish strip or squid strip.

CUCKOO RAY

The most distinctive species of the ray tribe, the cuckoo ray has a heart-shaped body and yellowish-brown back. To make positive identification even easier, this fish has a large, dark eye spot on each wing and each spot has yellow spots and wavy lines superimposed on it. Cuckoo ray reach a maximum weight of around 3lb. A comparatively rare species, the cuckoo is normally caught on worm bait, and most rod-caught fish are taken accidentally on baits intended for other fish. Seldom common, the cuckoo ray occurs all around the British Isles.

UNDULATE RAY

Sometimes called the painted or pop-art ray, the undulate ray is easily the most beautiful of British rays. The back of this fish is sandy coloured overlaid with dark lines and blotches. Common in the west of Ireland, the undulate ray is being taken in increasing numbers from the English Channel.

SMALL-EYED RAY

Popular with both boat and shore anglers, the small-eyed ray will come inshore after nightfall, offering beach fishermen the chance to catch a ray from the shore. Very much a fish of the south and south-west coastline, the small-eyed ray is seldom found in more northern areas.

It is similar in wing shape to the blonde ray, but the small-eyed ray has a paler yellow-brown body colour, this background colour being overlaid with pale spots and lines. These lines are most defined at the extremities of the wings, and the edges of the wing and tail are outlined in a brilliant white strip.

A fine thornback ray from Keyhaven, Hampshire. Thornbacks are the commonest of the ray family.

Blonde ray: a fish of the hard tides.

A typical day's uptide fishing – lots of ray and a solitary bass.

STING-RAY

Very much a localized species, sting-ray are most common in the Solent and off the muddy Essex coastline; occasional stragglers do occur elsewhere but these are rare. Sting-ray grow to a large size, possibly reaching a maximum weight of around 70lb, and many specimens in excess of 20lb are caught by shore anglers. Hardly an attractive fish, the sting-ray has a drab brown back with its underside being a mottled white-grey. The whole body is coated in a thick covering of slime. The long whip-like tail of this fish carries a jagged, bony spine which can cut like a knife, and this spine is also coated in venom which can cause wounds to fester very quickly. There was a time when anglers cut the tail off each ray they caught, but fortunately this barbaric treatment has now been discontinued.

Very much a summer species, sting-rays are mostly caught in June and July. Very large fish may take fish or squid bait, but most sting-rays prefer ragworm, crab or hermit crab baits. Fit only as a sporting species, all sting-ray should be returned alive to the sea.

COMMON SKATE

Sometimes called the grey or blue skate, the common skate can grow to weights well in excess of 200lb and commercial fishing records indicate that fish of 400lb have been caught. Widely distributed, this fish is most common in Scottish and Irish waters – Orkney, Mull, Strangford Lough and the west coast of Ireland are the big skate hot spots. The common skate has a greyish-brown back with an overlay of light blotches and small, dark spots. The underside is grey with dark streaks.

When uptide casting, the baited hook can be placed over one of the lead spikes. Once the trace hits the water the hook will drop clear.

Fig 32 Hook hung on a lead spike for uptide casting.

Very much a target species, a big common skate is an ambition that most anglers hope to achieve. Fortunately most anglers and charter boat skippers are conservation-minded and each big fish is handled carefully and returned alive to the sea. Tagging programs show that most of these fish survive to be caught again.

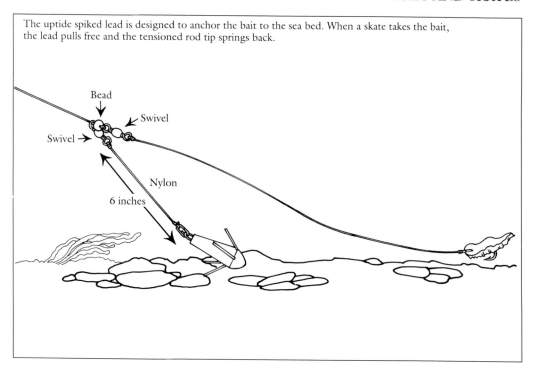

The uptide spiked lead is designed to anchor the bait to the sea bed. When a skate takes the bait, the lead pulls free and the tensioned rod tip springs back.

Bead

Swivel

Swivel →

Nylon

6 inches

Fig 33   The running leger in use.

Giant skate eat just about anything that swims or crawls over the sea bed. Fish, squid, scallops, crabs and lobsters are all a regular part of a skate's diet sheet. Like most big fish they prefer their food fresh and most of the large rod and line specimens are taken on freshly caught mackerel or coalfish.

FISHING METHODS

Shore Fishing for Ray

Small-eyed ray and the odd thornback will feed inshore after dark. The ideal night for fishing is when it is warm with little or no wind – heavy seas will keep the fish offshore in sheltered water. The ideal time is when a rising tide coincides with darkness as this will allow you to fish the tide as it comes up and goes down again.

Ray fishing is not an exacting sport and calls for standard beach casting tackle and a single-hook running ledger. A spiked lead should be used, the baited hook being hung on one of the wire spikes for casting purposes (see Fig 32). Once the tackle hits the water, the impact will dislodge the hook and allow the ledger to fish normally (see Fig 33). For this style of fishing a 30lb BS nylon trace and a size 4-0 or 6-0 O'Shaugnessy hook should be used. Sand eels or fresh fillet of pouting make the best baits for ray fishing from the shore. In the case of pouting the bait should be caught on site while blast-frozen sand eels can be bought beforehand. Remember that when a skate or ray flops down on a bait the rod tip

Never common, the undulate or 'pop art' ray is a welcome catch.

will indicate a heavy knock. Never strike at this first indication, but wait and give the fish time to get the bait into its mouth. The strike should only be made when the rod tip starts to pull over steadily – a clear indication that the fish has swallowed the bait and is moving off in search of more food.

Boat Fishing

The terminal rig for boat fishing is simply a beefed-up version of the ledger rig used for shore fishing. For the smaller species the trace can be made up of either 40lb BS wire or 100lb BS nylon; for giant common skate 100lb BS wire or 250lb BS long-liner nylon should be used. Skate and ray do not have teeth in the accepted sense of the word, but their bony lip plates and the power of their jaws can easily crush or sever lighter trace material. For the normal run of ray a 30lb or 50lb class outfit is ample, and for giant skate a 50lb or 80lb outfit should be used. Heavier rods are best used when strong tides dictate the use of heavy leads. For general boat fishing a 6-0 hook is large enough, but for giant skate a 8-0 or 10-0 Mustad Seamaster is the best choice.

It should be noted here that monkfish and angler fish may fall to baits presented on skate tackle.

Boating a 192lb common skate in the Orkneys.

9 *Tope*

The tope is a small member of the shark family. The fish has a typically shark-like appearance with prominent gill slits, two dorsal fins and a big tail which has a deeply notched upper lobe. Tope are greyish-white in colour with white underparts. Widely distributed, tope can be caught right around the British Isles, although northern fish seem to be heavier on average than southern tope.

FISHING METHODS

Shore Fishing

As with so many species, tope have suffered greatly from a lack of conservation which is particularly noticeable in the dramatic fall-off of shore-caught specimens. There was a time when tope could be caught from Solent beaches, north Cornish rock marks and the bays of west Wales. Today it is a rare occurrence to take such fish and many anglers have long since given up trying.

Tope are most likely to raid the shoreline during the months of June, July and August, a time when mackerel shoals sweep in to feed on sand eels and brill. Interestingly, most inshore tope are big females, the male fish preferring to group well offshore. Steep beaches or rock marks which fall away in to deep water are the places to try for these fish.

Terminal tackle should be kept to a simple running ledger baited with a whole small fish or half a large fish. Blast-frozen baits are now available in most good fishing tackle shops or, in the case of sardines, from the freezer section of a large supermarket. For this style of fishing a multiplying reel is preferable to even a large, fixed spool as bites are normally tear-away affairs. Never leave the tackle unguarded and with the reel in gear – a fast-moving tope operates on a hit-and-run basis and more than one unlucky angler has watched in horror as his expensive outfit has disappeared out to sea.

Boat Fishing

Tope fishing gives the average angler every opportunity to tangle with a fish that can and will put up a good fight. In the past

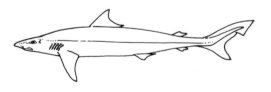

Tope.

quantity and in some areas vast packs are encountered. The area off St Catherine's Lighthouse on the Isle of Wight is a typical male tope stronghold – on a good day these grounds can produce thirty or forty fish, while a really good day can produce double this amount. Female tope are very different. Normally 'loners', the big females can top 50lb in weight and are more likely to show up in the shallower waters off the Essex coastline or in the sheltered waters of Northern Ireland's Strangford Lough. Tope can be found in many other areas, of course, but it is up to the angler to decide whether he wants quantity or quality and book his boat trips accordingly. The chosen area will also dictate the style of angling.

Tope seem to relish a hard flow of tide. Traditionally slack water was always considered the right time to fish, but as with most angling traditions this slack water theory was biased to the angler rather than the fish. Nowadays, of course, wire lines make it possible to fish right through heavy tides and this has resulted in more fish being boated than ever before.

Tope are basically bottom feeders that reap a harvest of pouting, flatfish, small pout and so on. However, on occasion they will feed close to the surface where they can make a nuisance of themselves by taking baits intended for shark. Top baits for tope are mackerel, horse mackerel and pouting, although at a pinch any fresh bait-sized fish will suffice. Stale baits hold little appeal for hungry tope – their lives are spent hunting down living fish and unless a bait is straight from the water it may go untouched. The choice of using a livebait or a freshly killed bait is up to the individual angler and when tope are feeding in packs either will work well. On days when the fish are finicky, however, a livebait will definitely outfish the freshest of deadbaits. Livebaits should be

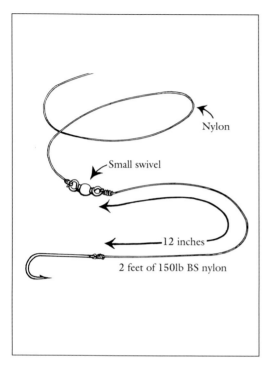

Fig 34   Uptide ledger for tope with 12 inches of wire.

tope have been described as the poor man's shark – a title which they richly deserve. A true shark in every sense of the word, the tope is a fast-moving game fish that on average equals or exceeds the average size of the blue shark caught off Britain's south-west coastlines. Hooked on reasonable tackle – for example, a 30lb class boat rod – even a comparatively small specimen can and will give a good account of itself. The decision that most boat anglers have to take is whether to fish for a really large tope or to be content with general tope fishing.

Male fish tend to be lighter than the females and at the outside may reach a weight of 50lb, although most males average 25–30lb. However, what the male fish lack in poundage they make up for in

A hooked tope makes its first serious bid for freedom.

Nigel Arkell of Fareham ready to return a 36lb tope.

Skipper and angler look pleased with this tope.

A nice tope ready to go back alive.

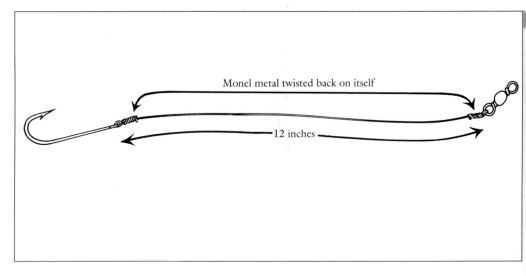

Monel metal twisted back on itself

12 inches

Fig 35   Tope hook link.

hooked once through the root of the tail as this gives a firm hookhold.

Up-tide Fishing

The Essex tope marks are mostly shallow water venues where the shadow or general vibration of an anchored boat causes the fish to shy away. For this reason up-tiding or boat casting is the favoured method of catching fish. The basic technique and tackle used in boat casting has already been

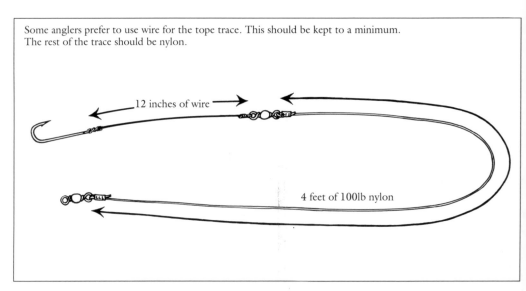

Some anglers prefer to use wire for the tope trace. This should be kept to a minimum. The rest of the trace should be nylon.

12 inches of wire

4 feet of 100lb nylon

Fig 36   Tope trace.

Tope must be conserved. To do this the fish should be lifted by the dorsal fin and tail.

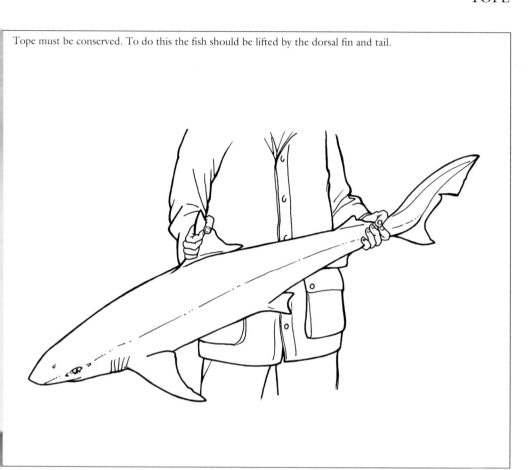

Fig 37   Handling tope.

described in an earlier chapter. The terminal tackle, however, needs a little explanation. Tope have sharp teeth and to avoid cut-offs the standard up-tide ledger rig should incorporate a 12in section of wire to which the hook is attached (see Fig 35). The standard nylon-covered wire is not reliable for tope or any type of shark fishing as the nylon sheathing has a tendency to catch on teeth and this allows the fish to saw through the wire core in seconds. The ideal wire for this leader is a 12in length of monel metal wire line which is tough, has little tendency to kink and can be twisted back on itself without needing crimps.

Tope Traces

For many years ultra-long wire traces were used for tope fishing and even today many anglers make and use traces which consist of two 3ft sections of wire. Such traces are tangle prone and totally outdated. Today's tope traces should be made up of 12in of wire and 4ft of 100lb BS long-liner nylon (see Fig 36).

A good-sized male tope makes quite a handful.

Terminal Tackle

A standard running ledger will suffice for most tope fishing situations. The heavy nylon of the trace acts as a rubbing leader; lighter trace material would chafe through on the shark's skin.

Handling Tope

Conservation is now a byword with tope anglers and skippers alike. Fish are caught for sport, handled carefully and returned alive to the water. Gaffs should not be used, and instead the fish should be tailed or, better still, lifted into the boat by the tail and dorsal fin (see Fig 37). To keep the fish from thrashing about it should turned belly up – fish handled in this way normally remain passive while the hook is removed. If a fish is deep hooked the trace should be snipped off as close to the hook as possible.

CONSERVATION .

Due to over fishing, tope stocks have dwindled to an all-time low. This over fishing plus a marked rise in inshore pollution practically wiped the fish out. The pollution is unfortunately still there. Anglers, however, now understand that tope are a sporting rather than an eating fish. The bad old days when huge numbers of tope were killed are thankfully over. Today's thinking sea angler prefers to guestimate the weight of his catch. The fish can then be unhooked, photographed, and carefully returned alive, perhaps to be caught again by some other lucky angler.

During the past decade, this awareness on the part of anglers has done much to re-establish the tope stocks to something of the old levels. Today's fish are young and growing. Maybe they don't weigh as much as they once did. This will change as the fish live on to reach maturity. Long may this trend continue. Even a big tope may not be a monster, but for many it will be the largest fish they ever catch.

10 *Mackerel and Garfish*

Every sea angler must be familiar with the mackerel. Hard hitting and almost suicidal on occasions, these game little fish can be found right around the British Isles.

Basically a summer species, the mackerel shoals move well offshore during the cold winter months. Totally predatory, mackerel are fish eaters, feeding off the fry of herring, sprat, pilchard and many other species although during late spring they may also feed on banks of drifting plankton.

Most rod-caught mackerel weigh 1–2lb and occasionally fish weighing over 4lb are taken. Pound for pound the mackerel is one of the gamest fighting fish on the British list.

Mackerel.

The elongated garfish is another fighting species often found with the shoaling mackerel. With its long, slim body and birdlike bill, the garfish looks like a diminutive member of the marlin family.

Unlike the mackerel which fights deep, the garfish spends as much time out of the water as it does in it. Garfish also have a wide distribution range, but are probably most common along the southern and south western coastlines of the British Isles. Garfish have green bones which puts many people off them as a table species and this is a pity for they make first-class eating.

Mackerel feed at all levels whereas the garfish are essentially surface hunters. The exception to this is during excessively rough weather when they may resort to bottom feeding. Both species can be caught from boats and techniques are basically the same no matter what the venue.

FISHING METHODS

Spinning

Both mackerel and garfish are attracted by small artificial baits although the garfish, with its narrow beak, is more difficult to hook than the relatively large-mouthed mackerel. Neither species is fussy about types of lures – whether the artificial spins, wobbles, vibrates or flutters it will catch both species. Both species like a fast-moving bait and for this reason it is best to retrieve the lure at high speed. The lighter the tackle the greater the sport.

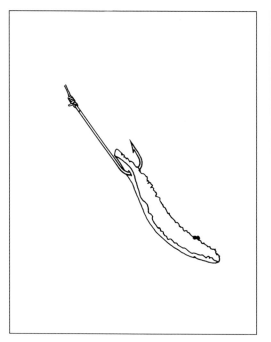

Fig 38   A strip of mackerel is a great bait for other mackerel.

Drift-line Fishing

For pier, harbour or small boat fishing, drift-line tackle can be used effectively against both mackerel and garfish. Only the lightest of tackle should be used for this technique. The best bait is a 4in long and ½–¾in wide sliver of skin from the belly of a fresh mackerel or garfish. To work properly the bait should be hooked once through the pointed end (see Fig 38).

The object of drift-lining is to use the tidal flow to carry the bait along gently and at the most a single split shot should be used (see Fig 39). Once cast out the angler must hold the rod at all times – a small fixed-spool reel with the bale arm in the open position is best used for this style of angling. Tiny portions of chopped fish can be thrown

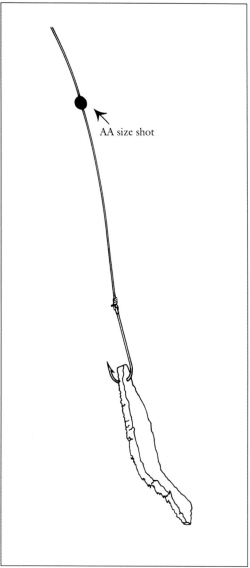

Fig 39   Use of a split shot when drift lining.

out to attract and hold the attention of the shoaling fish. Freshwater hooks in sizes 6 or 8 are ideal for this style of angling. Bites are normally tear-away affairs which are difficult to miss on the strike.

81

Mackerel caught on red-gill sandeel.

Russell Housby pleased with his garfish catch.

By adding a single shot, 6–8 inches from the hook bait, the bait can be given 'life' on the retrieve. Size of shot depends on the strength of the tide.

Fig 40 Retrieving a drift line.

Float Fishing

Where tides are strong, float fishing can be an excellent way of taking fish. Mackerel change feeding levels throughout the day and for this reason a streamlined sliding float should be employed. When bites cease, the float stop can be moved up or down until the feeding level is relocated. Garfish are easier to fish for as basically they are a surface feeding species, and the float can be set at 2–5ft without the angler having to worry about changing it as feeding levels change. Fish or squid strips or a section of ragworm can be used as bait.

When retrieving the bait never wind at speed. Instead turn the reel handle slowly and stop at regular intervals so that the bait swings up in an attractive manner (see Fig 40). Bites can come at any time during the retrieve and biting mackerel generally drag the float straight under. Garfish may play with the bait, making the float bob up and down before it can get the bait into its narrow jaws. The only shape of weight that lends itself to this style of angling is a barrel lead. These should be carried in ½oz sizes – a float that requires more weight is too large for mackerel and garfish.

Feathering for Mackerel

When mackerel are shoaling a set of feathers can be deadly (see Fig 41). Used over the side of a boat or cast out and wound back at speed, feathers can produce large catches of mackerel. There is little sport to be had from catching mackerel six at a time, however, this technique is a useful way of catching bait. Anglers often become greedy, outdoing each other to fill bag after bag with fish. This is a bad practice as mackerel go off quickly in warm weather and a big catch at the start of the day is only fit for

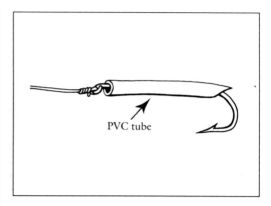

Fig 42 PVC tubing as a stronger replacement for feathers.

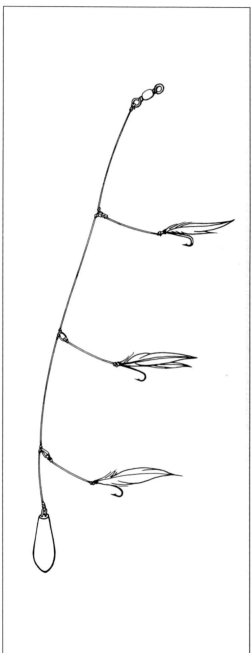

Fig 41 Feathers are a standard mackerel lure, particularly effective when the fish are shoaling.

dumping at the end of the day. It is better to catch the fish at the end of the trip as such a catch will then arrive home in good shape. Nowadays a wide range of mackerel feathers are available. All of these catch fish, but they tend to be torn to shreds quickly by the striking and struggling fish. When this occurs the feathers or flectolite bodies can be replaced by coloured sections of PVC tubing (see Fig 42) – this will catch fish just as well as the most elaborate feathers.

Five nice grey mullet from the breakwater on Alderney.

A nice catch of grey mullet caught on tiny pieces of pork meat.

11 *Mullet*

Four types of mullet are found in British waters – three types of grey mullet, and the rare and diminutive red mullet. Only the grey mullet are of interest to the angler. These are the thin-lipped, the thick-lipped and the golden-grey mullet, the golden-grey mullet having distinctive golden cheek patches. The average size of rod-caught mullet is 1½–3lb, while any mullet over 5lb is a good catch.

Mullet.

Mullet are shoal fish. The largest shoals are normally made up of the smaller fish while large mullet tend to swim in small groups. They are a southern species and are common from the Thames estuary around to north Devon. Some of the greatest concentrations of mullet are found in the Channel Islands, and the west coast of

Ireland is also a good place to catch these elusive fish.

In their natural state mullet feed on algae and soft mud from which they extract a variety of aquatic organisms, but as a species they quickly learn to scavenge. Channel Island anglers use meat scraps to catch their mullet, and bread, cheese, macaroni, banana and many other household foods can be used to catch fish. No matter what they feed on mullet never lose their shyness and inbred caution, and this has given them a justifiable reputation for being practically uncatchable. However, the angler who applies himself to the problems can soon learn to catch these lovely fish.

TACKLE

Sea tackle has no place in mullet fishing; heavy rods and thick lines are a recipe for disaster. Instead, freshwater tackle is essential. The ideal outfit is a 1lb test curve tench rod 11–12ft in length. This should be matched to a medium-sized fixed-spool reel loaded with 5lb BS line. Remember, however, that salt water is corrosive, so you should wash your tackle in fresh water and dry it with a lightly oiled cloth.

Floats

Sea floats are useless for mullet fishing. Highly sensitive to any drag, mullet will

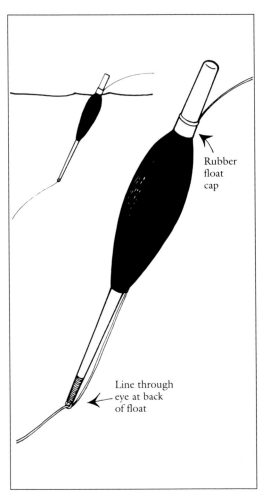

Rubber
float
cap

Line through
eye at back
of float

Fig 43 A trotting float.

Lines

A quality monofilament line of 5lb BS is about right for mullet fishing. For float fishing the line should be greased thoroughly with line floatant before use – this allows the line to float on the surface making for faster and easier striking. Most tackle shops stock line grease and a tin will last for many seasons.

Hooks

Sea hooks are far too large for mullet fishing. It is better to carry a range of freshwater scale hooks in sizes 6, 8, 10, 12 and 14. The new chemically sharpened hooks are perfect for hard-mouthed fish like mullet.

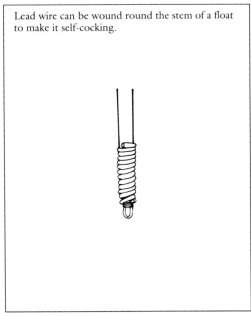

Lead wire can be wound round the stem of a float to make it self-cocking.

drop a bait presented beneath a bulky float. The ideal floats to use are freshwater trotting floats (see Fig 43) which are made of balsa or clear plastic. A range of such floats should be carried at all times. On calm days the lightest pattern should be used while in rough conditions the heaviest float in the range may be essential. The floats should be attached at both ends.

Fig 44 A self-cocking float.

The author's son mullet fishing in Lymington marina.

Landing Nets

For boat fishing within easy reach of the water, a standard landing net can be used; when fishing from harbour walls or piers a drop net is essential.

Additional Tackle

A box of BB split shot, some small barrel swivels and a coil of fine lead wire should always be carried. The lead wire is useful when the mullet show interest in a free-falling bait. By winding a length of wire around the float stem (see Fig 44) the float can be turned into a self-cocking model which will allow the bait to drop at a natural speed through the water. For bottom fishing a range of bomb-shaped leads weighing ¼–¾oz should be carried. Always ensure that

you have plenty of shot, wire, leads, swivels and hooks as these small items can easily be lost and a day's fishing will be ruined.

BAITS

Grey mullet are opportunist feeders. Provided that enough bait samples are introduced to a given area, these fish adjust quickly to the new style of food. Bread has accounted for a great many big mullet and as a bait it is very versatile. It can be made into a paste, and can be flavoured and coloured to suit the angler and the fish. Bread can be used in crust form as a surface bait or it can be used as simple flake which is the crumb of a newly baked loaf. To use it properly, a thumbnail-sized piece of flake should be pinched off the loaf. This should

Safe at last. A 6¾lb mullet brought up in a drop net.

Mullet often like a bait which falls naturally through the water. To achieve the free fall, the shot should be bunched underneath the float. If the fish are definitely bottom-feeding, the shot should be 6–8 inches from the hook.

Fig 45 Self-cocking float.

then be folded and pinched around the shank of the hook. The bread covering the bend and barb of the hook should be left fluffy – never pinch the bread all over as it will harden in the water and become too tough to pull the hook through on the strike. Various cheeses can also be used with success, and macaroni, tinned peas, banana and raw meat are all productive mullet baits. Harbour ragworm can also be effective.

Groundbait or Shirvy

Groundbait or shirvy is an essential part of successful mullet fishing. Top mullet anglers have their own secret recipes which usually work on a fish or meat-based flavour. A typical shirvy consists of finely minced meat and bran, mixed with animal blood. A good shirvy is made up of loose consistency – if it is too solid it will sink in a lump.

The whole trick of attracting mullet is to underfeed rather than overfeed. A wooden spoon quarter filled contains an ample amount of bait particles, and this quantity should be flicked out every fifteen minutes or so. Once mullet lock on to a stream of shirvy they normally follow it back to source, and once the fish can be seen, fishing can commence.

FISHING METHODS

Float Fishing

When mullet fishing the float is used mainly to support the bait at a given depth. Few anglers actually use the float as a bite indicator. Instead they watch the actual bait and strike when a fish appears to take it. Obviously in cloudy water this is not possible, but most mullet are caught in clear water where bait watching is fairly simple.

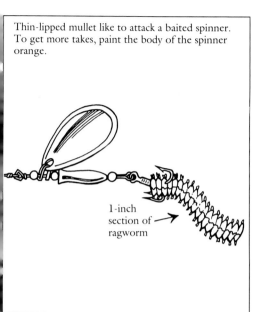

Thin-lipped mullet like to attack a baited spinner. To get more takes, paint the body of the spinner orange.

1-inch section of → ragworm

Fig 46 A baited bar spoon.

The float depth should be set to the depth at which mullet can be seen feeding. In fast tidal areas the split shot should be bunched to take the bait down quickly (see Fig 45). Where slacker tides prevail the shot can be placed directly under the float – this allows the bait to drop naturally through the water.

Bottom Fishing

Sometimes pier mullet will feed close to the bottom. Under these circumstances a simple nylon paternoster should be used. Bites are then felt for by holding the line in the left hand, or they can be detected by watching the rod top. Mullet are quick to clean a hook, so the strike must be made the second a bite occurs.

Spinning

Where thin-lipped grey mullet occur they can be caught in quantity on a tiny, baited bar spoon (see Fig 46), and the best bait to use for this is a tiny section of ragworm. To be really effective, a mullet spinner should have a touch of bright orange about it. Spinning is a nice method for catching mullet and allows the angler to fish with a light rod and line. Bites are solid affairs and most of the fish are hooked on impact.

Free-lining

Occasionally mullet will feed on the surface. Under these circumstances a thumbnail-sized section of bread crust can be a deadly bait. The crust should be dipped in the water to add weight for casting purposes – once wet it can be cast quite long distances. Never use this bait when there is a chance of hooking a seagull.

Although mullet can often be obliging fish, easily sighted as they cruise on to the surface, they can also be secretive as well. Many a local angler with a lifetime's area experience has been shocked to discover that he has been sitting on shoals of mullet without the slightest idea of their presence. Often his first insight into a hitherto local mullet population comes when a visiting angler makes a big catch. Such is the fascination of mullet. A species around which a thriving club has been established, a species which still has the reputation of being the hardest fish on the list to catch.

Following page: a blue shark comes to the boat.

12 *Sharks*

Of the four types of shark found in British waters only the blue and the porbeagle sharks are common enough to be taken on a regular basis. The mako and the thresher sharks can be caught, but only in limited numbers and both of these fish tend to be taken by accident on baits intended for the two more common species. All four species are active hunters living on shoal fish such as mackerel, herring, codling and similar species. The thresher shark also shows a marked interest in flatfish. Porbeagle and thresher sharks are probably resident throughout the year, while mako and blue sharks are more migratory, drifting in from the Atlantic during the summer months. Neither of the latter two species show a liking for low water temperatures. In a good year both may stay until mid-October, but when the autumn weather is cold and blustery they may vanish a month earlier. It is interesting to note that during February 1991 a Scottish commercial boat caught 189 porbeagle sharks, proof that these fish live and thrive in cold water conditions.

FEEDING HABITS

All four British sharks are active hunters and may overlap on food-rich areas. Normally, however, each shark species has its preference for particular areas. Blue shark, for example, are an offshore species which like a lot of deep water and seldom venture into inshore waters. The major Cornish blue shark grounds are located between ten and twenty miles from the shore. Despite its racy appearance, the blue shark is at best a sluggish fish content to feed on live or dead fish. Most of its food consists of pilchards, sprats and whatever mackerel it can pick up. Blue shark probably respond to rubby dubby (see page 97) better than any other British shark and will also take soft baits that most shark would pass up.

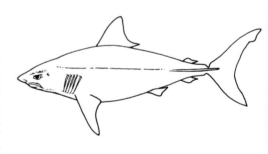

Porbeagle shark.

In contrast to the blue shark, the chunky porbeagle is a raider. It is a fast moving shark which is at home in both inshore and offshore waters – off north Devon and Ireland these pack sharks are often found close in to the cliffs. Blue sharks may or may not swim in company with others of their own kind, but porbeagles are definitely pack

96

fish which hunt in groups. Porbeagle shark like fast tides, overfalls and other disturbed areas of water. It would seem that porbeagle use the tide races as a feeding aid – mackerel shoals which swim into overfall areas seem to become disorientated, making them fall easy prey to the smash-and-grab techniques of the porbeagle packs. Porbeagle will also use large wrecks as feeding areas and many a big cod or pollack has been ripped off by a hungry porbeagle. If the angler is lucky he may get half of his fish and all of his terminal tackle back, but on the other hand he may lose both the fish and his end tackle.

The mako shark is a very different proposition. A loner by inclination, the mako is an oceanic wanderer that likes to feed near islands and isolated rock stacks. In the West Country most shark boats fish too far offshore for successful mako fishing. Thirty years ago when Falmouth was the mako port most of the fish came from the area off the dreaded Manacles rocks, and the long-held 500lb record mako was taken from an area inside the Eddystone Reef. By inclination the mako is a swashbuckler, a fish which is frightened of nothing and which spends its life hunting. These shark like live fish and big baits, and although the odd few have been caught or hooked on blue shark baits of pilchard or mackerel, these fish can be classed as accidental catches. The ideal bait for a mako is a 5–7lb pollack. Such a fish should be presented alive or at least freshly killed as mako are hunters and not scavengers. If you fish with anything but the best baits you deserve what you catch, which will not be much.

The thresher shark with its massive tail is more common than most anglers realize, and also grows to huge sizes. The reason that giant thresher are rarely caught is that normally these fish frequent inshore waters of moderate depth. They prefer a sandy sea bed where they feed mainly on flatfish. The few that are caught each season are normally accidental catches taken on conventional shark techniques. Thresher shark mostly hunt in pairs. The extremely long tail lobe of this fish is used to churn up the water to confuse and terrify food fish. Although they feed mainly on flatfish and whiting, when mackerel and herring shoals are thick they will take advantage of this easy food supply. To a certain extent they must also feed on shoaling sand eels as they often snatch at a string of mackerel feathers. Obviously a big shark hooked on mackerel tackle soon makes good its escape, but they do tend to jump several times before chewing through the nylon line. The thresher shark and savage mako are jumping fish while porbeagles and blue shark never make an attempt to jump. The mako jumps higher than the thresher, but both fish are impressive leapers.

ATTRACTING SHARK

Shark hunt by scent more than by sight. For this reason they can be attracted by an established smell lane. Most shark fishing is done from a drifting boat which allows the anglers to cover as much ground as possible during the course of a day's fishing. To create the smell lane required to bring shark to the boat, a pungent mixture of minced fish, bran and fish oil is mixed – this is known as rubby dubby. Once mixed, this groundbait is scooped into a mesh onion sack and hung over the side of the boat. The natural rise and fall of the waves causes the sack to slap on the sea surface and a constant trickle of bait particles is washed out. The oil-soaked particles quickly form a bait trail that spreads as it flows away. To be effective the bag must be kept topped up at all times.

The skipper holds the leader to control a big porbeagle shark.

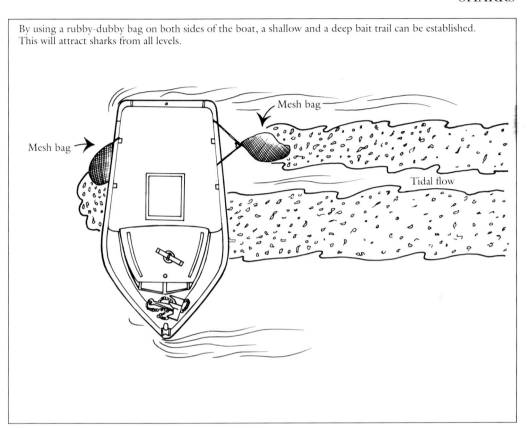

By using a rubby-dubby bag on both sides of the boat, a shallow and a deep bait trail can be established. This will attract sharks from all levels.

Mesh bag

Mesh bag

Tidal flow

Fig 47 Using a rubby-dubby bag.

It is impossible to overdo the amount of dubby used, the whole idea being to attract but not feed any shark that pick up the trail. In only a few hours this enticing smell lane may be several miles long and any shark that comes into contact with it will normally turn into it and follow it to its source. On calm days the fish can be seen cruising on the surface faithfully following the bait trail.

By hanging the mesh bag on the up-tide side of the boat a shallow trail can be laid; by positioning the bag on the opposite side the bait particles are washed down and under the keel of the drifting boat. This shoots the bait trail down into the depths, hopefully bringing deep-feeding fish up to the bait level. To lay a solid bait trail two bags can be attached as illustrated (see Fig 47). The best rubby dubby is made with naturally oily fish such as mackerel, horse mackerel, herring and sprat. Where possible fish oil should be used to mix the minced fish flesh and bran – pilchard oil is best but cod oil is an easily obtainable substitute.

FISHING METHODS

To get the best out of drift fishing for shark, baits should be set at staggered depths. Most shark anglers use partially inflated balloons as floats (see Fig 48) which should

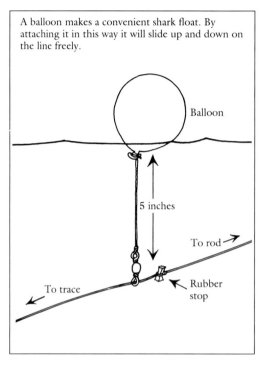

A balloon makes a convenient shark float. By attaching it in this way it will slide up and down on the line freely.

Balloon

5 inches

To rod

To trace

Rubber stop

Fig 48 A balloon float.

be attached to the reel line by sewing thread. When the fish takes the bait and dives, water pressure against the balloon will normally cause the thread to snap thus leaving the fish to fight naturally. Balloon floats should be inflated to the size of a large orange, and round balloons make the best floats – elongated balloons do not sit correctly in the water and may cause the tackle to twist and tangle. Normally four rods are fished each with its float set at a different level, say 20ft, 30ft, 50ft and 60ft. This lays a curtain of baits which should attract shark from all levels. On calm days it is usually the shallow-set baits that catch fish, and when seas are rough the deep-set baits normally produce all the action.

SHARK TRACES

The most critical part of a shark outfit is the trace and the hook. Far too many anglers lose fish by using inferior trace materials and

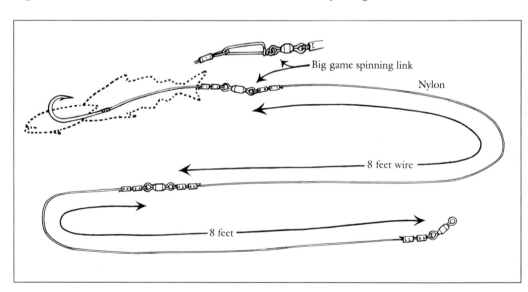

Big game spinning link

Nylon

8 feet wire

8 feet

Fig 49 Shark trace.

The first section of a shark trace should be of wire. The second section should be heavy nylon.
This makes the trace easier to handle.

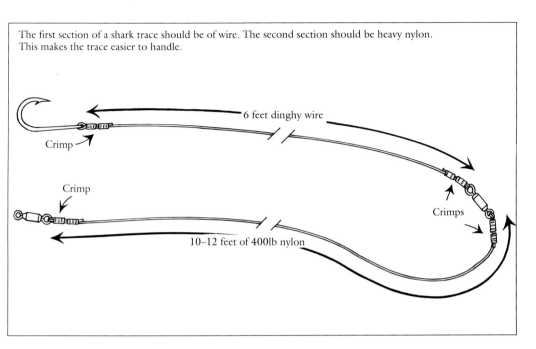

Crimp

6 feet dinghy wire

Crimp

Crimps

10–12 feet of 400lb nylon

Fig 50   Shark trace.

Shark like a big bait. A favourite is two mackerel,
one dead, the other tail-hooked and alive.

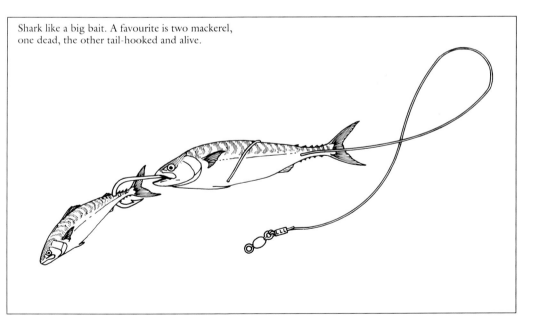

Fig 51   Double mackerel bait for shark.

the wrong type of hook. A shark trace should be 16ft long and made up from two equal sections of galvanized dinghy rigging wire. Each section is joined by a large Berkley-style barrel swivel (see Fig 49). Never use ordinary brass swivels as these may fall apart under heavy action. For those anglers who prefer to limit the amount of trace wire, a good alternative is to use 6ft of dinghy wire and 10ft of crimped long-liner nylon of 400lb BS (see Fig 50). If a hooked shark does roll up in the trace the tough nylon will not part when it comes into contact with the shark's abrasive skin. If you use a big game spring link (see Fig 49) it can quickly be unclipped when the shark is in the boat so that a new trace can be attached – this saves the problem of extracting hooks from a live shark. Obviously, however, if shark are being returned the wire can be cut and hook lost.

When it comes to hooks only one pattern should be considered. This is the Mustad Seamaster, size 10-0 or 12-0. The Seamaster is a very strong hook with an offset point, and once well sharpened it sets easily on the strike and will take a great deal of punishment.

BAIT

Shark of all types like large, fresh baits. The easiest bait to obtain and use is a pair of good sized mackerel. These should be attached carefully to the hook (see Fig 51). This double bait creates a large looking shiny bait which few shark can resist. The tail mackerel is hooked just once through the wrist of the tail – if a taking shark chews this fish off it will normally come back for the second, well-wrapped bait.

13 *Wrasse*

Five or six species of wrasse are found around the British coastline but only two of them, the cuckoo wrasse and the ballan wrasse, are of interest to anglers.

The brightly coloured cuckoo wrasse is a deep-water species normally caught by accident. The ballan wrasse is a shallow-water fish which provides excellent sport for shore and small boat fishermen. Ballan wrasse, which can reach weights of 10lb, are noted for their strength and tenacity when hooked. The coloration of the ballan wrasse is rich and variable, the most common colours being brown or greeny-brown. Large specimens are often very green or orange-red in colour. Wrasse are of little use as a table fish and should be caught simply for sport. If handled with respect wrasse can

A typical ballan wrasse from a deep rock gully.

easily be returned alive to the sea, however, some anglers unfortunately regard them as bait robbers and kill them accordingly. Ballan wrasse often provide young anglers with their first catch, a catch that can give them a lifelong love of angling.

FEEDING HABITS

Cuckoo wrasse are normally caught on fish strips or worm baits, usually being taken by accident rather than intent. Ballan wrasse feed mainly on crustacea, molluscs and marine worms, and small hard-backed crabs (preferably alive) make the best hookbait. The best method of attaching crabs to a

hook is as follows: turn the crab on its back, and push the hook point through the triangle at the base of its shell, making certain that the hook point and barb protrude through the crab's back shell (see Fig 52). Hard-backed crabs are easy to collect at low tide and can be kept in a bait can half-filled with damp seaweed. Worm baits catch plenty of wrasse, particularly the smaller fish, while crab baits are more selective.

For shallow work a float should be attached at both ends.

Hard-backed crab should be hooked from the underside. This presents them right-side up.

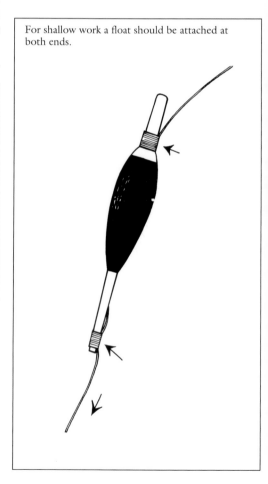

Fig 52   Hooking crab for wrasse.

Fig 53   Fixed float.

FISHING METHODS

Float Fishing

Wrasse are a rock-dwelling species showing a particular liking for life in deep rock gullies. They seem to prefer the type of gully which partially dries out at low water. For float fishing it is best to choose a gully which has a comparatively level bottom as the bait can then be set to fish 6–8in above the sea bed. Depending on the depth of a gully either a fixed or sliding float can be used (see Figs 52 and 56).

Fig 54 Using a paternoster for wrasse.

A pretty little ballan wrasse.

Wrasse of this size take worm or limpet.

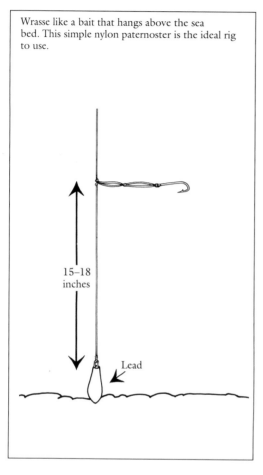

Wrasse like a bait that hangs above the sea bed. This simple nylon paternoster is the ideal rig to use.

15–18 inches

Lead

Fig 55 Correct distance from the hook link to lead.

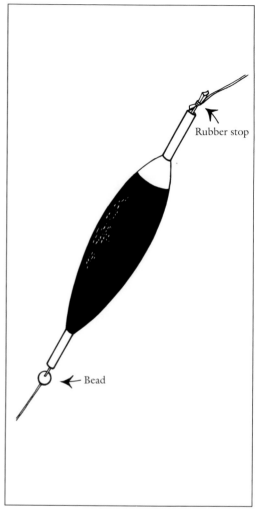

Rubber stop

Bead

Fig 56 A sliding float.

Wrasse bite in a distinctive manner and normally the float will bob two or three times before sliding rapidly out of sight. Once hooked, a large wrasse will dive instinctively for cover. To prevent the fish going to ground it is essential that you apply maximum pressure from the start. The first run of a hooked wrasse is the most dangerous, but once this has been countered the fish will normally come quickly to the net.

Bottom Fishing

Although some anglers do use a running ledger rig for wrasse fishing a single-hook paternoster rig is far more suitable. Wrasse live over ragged and often weed-infested bottoms, and the ledger has a tendency to snag up over such ground. The paternoster rig, however, is far more reliable and gullies

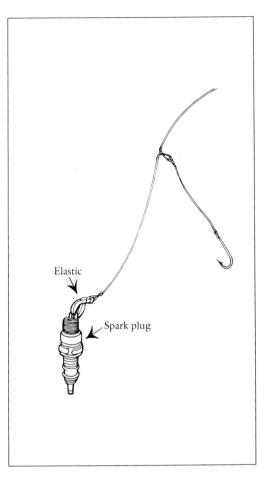

Fishing Tip

Weights have to be expendable for wrasse fishing. The very nature of the rugged terrain in which these fish live and feed dictates that lead losses are high. To cut costs many anglers use spark plugs or links of heavy chain – both make a perfect substitute for shop-bought leads. Spark plugs or chain links can be attached by an elastic band (see Fig 57) – if the weight becomes snagged, heavy pressure will snap the band and release the remaining terminal tackle. Over a season's fishing this can save quite a few pennies.

Elastic

Spark plug

Fig 57 A trip to the local garage can yield plenty of old spark plugs. This can cut the cost of fishing the sort of rough ground wrasse like. The plug can be attached by a rubber band or garden tie. These will pull out if the plug gets snagged.

which have deep holes and shallow areas are perfect for this style of angling. If the bait is worked off the shallows into a deep area it is only necessary to release a little line to fish the bait at the correct height off the sea bed (see Fig 54).

A wrasse paternoster is made by doubling up the reel line and knotting the resulting loop to form a semi-stiff nylon boom with the hook hanging freely at the end (see Fig 55). This boom should be 8–9in long, and the tail of reel line between the weight and boom should be 15–18in long as this allows the baited hook to hang in the area where hunting wrasse expect to find food. This paternoster rig can be used for both shore and boat fishing.

Rob la Ballastair and a 7lb 12oz Alderney wrasse taken on crab bait.

Rock anglers fishing at a typical bass and wrasse mark.

14 *Pollack and Coalfish*

Pollack and coalfish provide good sport to rock and harbour anglers alike. Pollack are common in southern waters while coalfish are common in northern seas, but offshore it is a different story. West Country wrecks throw up good catches of both fish, and these deepwater wreck specimens grow to weights well in excess of 20lb. Inshore fish are much smaller, rarely exceeding 3lb in weight.

move back to feed in the really rugged areas again. Over inshore marks the fish seldom stray far from rocks or harbour walls. During the autumn months inshore stocks are occasionally increased by an influx of larger fish which often exceed 10lb in weight. Obviously such fish move in to take full advantage of a food-rich area before heading out to the offshore marks where they spend the winter months.

Pollack.

Pollack and coalfish are reef, rock or wreck fish which rarely stray on to the open sea bed. Both species are inclined to change their feeding grounds throughout the season. During the spring and early summer they tend to hug the rock pinnacles and upthrust wreckage. Later, as the season progresses, they move out to feed over rough and stony ground, and then as winter approaches they

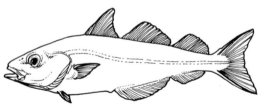

Coalfish.

IDENTIFICATION

Many anglers find it difficult to distinguish between the two species, but once you know what to look for identification is simple. The two give-away points are the

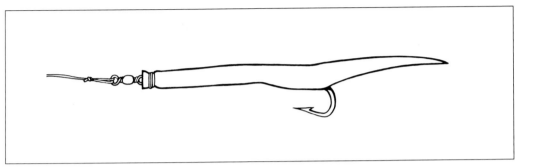

Fig 58   Simple rubber eel.

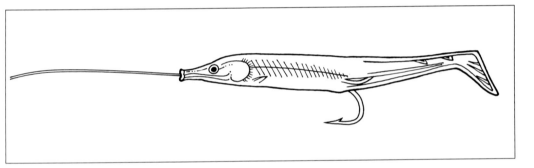

Fig 59   Red-gill Eddystone-type eel.

lower jaw and the lateral lines. The lower jaw of the pollack projects beyond the upper jaw and the lateral line is dark, while the lower jaw of the coalfish either recedes or is the same length as the upper jaw and its lateral line is light and almost dirty white in colour. The body colour of both fish can vary greatly from one locality to the next, but the brightest colours are normally found on fish which live in comparatively shallow water. Generally the coalfish is a darker colour than the pollack. In West Country waters pollack which are covered in dark specks occur and are called locally 'tea makers'. Both fish grow to weights well in excess of 20lb although on average coalfish are larger than pollack and can top 33lb in weight.

FEEDING HABITS

Pollack and coalfish are fast, active hunters. Most of their food consists of small fish and eels which they catch alive. Both species indulge in cannibalism and will strike at any fish which is small enough to eat. Pollack, and to a lesser extent coalfish, will also scavenge – many big winter pollack are caught on squid or cut fish baits intended for cod or other large bottom feeders. Young pollack and coalfish will also take worm or fish strip baits

Pollack and coalfish taken on pirk and muppet.

Pollack fishing on Alderney.

presented on float tackle. Both species take artificial baits well, and in inshore waters both will take spinners or feathers.

FISHING METHODS

Trolling

Around rocky cliffs and islands, trolled artificial baits account for many specimens of both species. In fact, trolling was the traditional method used by the old harbour fishermen. In those days the bait was invariably a simple rubber eel cut from a section of rubber tubing (see Fig 58) and mounted on a special twisted shank hook which made the rubber tubing spin slowly. Nowadays rubber or plastic eels are still used, but they are faithful replicas of living sand eels which incorporate a waved tail (see Fig 59) that gives the bait every appearance of a rapidly swimming sand eel. In areas where heavy tides prevail it is sometimes advisable to use wire lines to get the baits down to the level of the fish – these lines allow the use of comparatively light lead weights.

Float Fishing

Both pollack and coalfish can be caught on float tackle, and this method works well from rock marks and harbour walls. The float should be set to fish below the mid-water mark. Both pollack and coalfish will rise almost to the surface during the twilight period, but during daylight hours they prefer to swim and feed in deeper water. Sliding float tackle is best for this style of

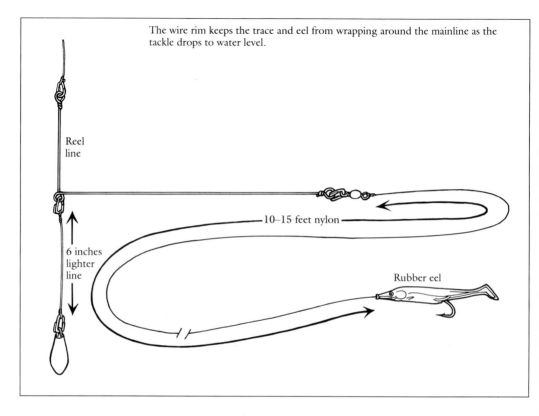

The wire rim keeps the trace and eel from wrapping around the mainline as the tackle drops to water level.

Reel line

10–15 feet nylon

6 inches lighter line

Rubber eel

Fig 60   Flying collar rig with an artificial lure.

fishing as the float stop can be adjusted as the tides rise and fall.

Most inshore pollack and coalfish weigh less than 3lb and for fish of this size a freshwater hook in size 2 or 4 will suffice for both worm, squid or fish strip baits. Both fish are bold feeders that normally take a bait with a rush, so float sizes should be kept to a minimum. Many perfect sliding floats can be bought from the freshwater section of the local tackle shop. Ideal sliding floats have a central tube through which the line runs easily – this style of float rarely tangles during casting.

Drift-Line Fishing

Although not widely used now, drift-line fishing can be a deadly way of taking reef pollack. As its name implies, drift-line tackle is designed to drift the bait at the prevailing speed of the tidal flow. At its simplest, drift-line tackle consists of a rod, reel, line and hook, the weight of the bait, worm or live sand eel being sufficient to take the bait down to the level of the fish. In strong tides a few heavy split shot can be added to get the bait down. Where possible additional lead of this type should be avoided as it tends to hamper the natural movement of

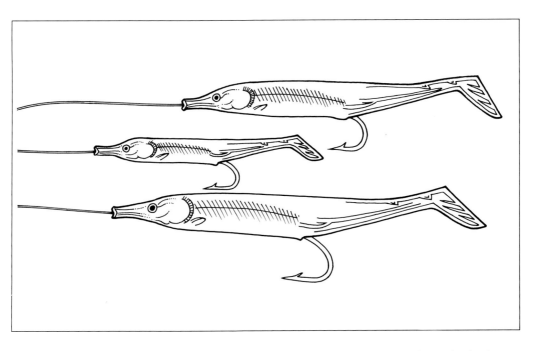

Fig 61 Always carry a range of artificial eels. The preferred colour and size can change by the day.

the bait, and this is essentially a light tackle method.

Wreck Fishing with Artificial Lures

Deep-water wrecks invariably produce the largest pollack and coalfish. The majority of these fish are taken on artificial sand eels. Red-gill eels and the less perfectly moulded Eddystone eels take the most big fish and big catches made in the United Kingdom. The technique is simple, and uses a wire boom known as a flying collar (see Fig 60). The long arm of this boom is designed to stop the trace from tangling as the tackle plummets down to the level of the wreck. The nylon trace between boom and lead should be at least 10ft although many anglers use far longer traces. The lead is lowered down until it bumps on the

bottom. The reel handle is then turned at high speed to bring the rubber eel racing up out of the wreck. Normally the eel is brought to the mid-water mark, and if a bite does not occur the rig is lowered down and the process repeated. Bites are normally slamming affairs that pull the rod tip hard down as the racing fish engulfs the eel.

Artificial eels should be carried in a range of colours and sizes (see Fig 61). Pollack and coalfish change their size and colour preferences by the day – one day an orange eel will work and the next a red or purple eel. When fish are being finicky the smallest eel may be the only one that brings bites.

Combining Lures

Many wreck anglers like to hedge their bets by using a combination of lures in the hope

117

of tempting cod and pollack or coalfish. A typical terminal rig is a pirk-style bait plus two red-gill eels fished on short droppers (see Fig 62). This sort of tackle is worked by raising and lowering the rod top. Occasionally this can be a deadly style of fishing, but like most combination rigs it can also fail miserably. On new wrecks where the fish are not wary of bait this sort of rig can produce more than the angler has banked on – a big cod or ling on the pirk plus a brace of pollack or coalfish can be a formidable combination. The power of three big fish hooked simultaneously can easily break the reel line, leaving the fish to die a slow and unpleasant death. It is therefore better to limit the tackle to one pirk and one artificial eel – two good fish can be controlled but three may be impossible to stop.

LIGHT TACKLE

With the general fall off of fish stocks due to wreck and inshore nets anglers now think in terms of sport rather than huge numbers of fish. This has led to the introduction of lighter tackle. The 30 and 50 pound class rods being ousted by lighter, longer rods of the up-tide type. This sort of outfit will handle a solitary big fish well.

It doesn't have the stamina for two or more big fish at one time. By taking single fish on lighter tackle, the average angler is getting more sport out of his fishing and automatically limiting his catch to a reasonable level. This helps both pollack and coalfish to maintain their numbers. Hopefully, this trend will continue.

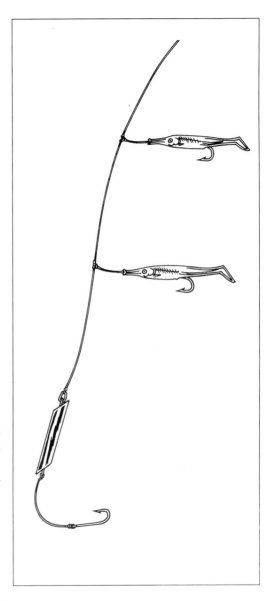

Fig 62 Combination of pirk and artificial eels.

Opposite: a prize pollack.

15 *Dogfish*

Few anglers enjoy catching dogfish. Competition anglers find them useful to make up weights in contests, but most regard them as little more than bait robbers.

GREATER AND LESSER SPOTTED DOGFISH

Of these two common species the greater spotted or bull huss grows the largest. Very much a rough ground species, the bull huss

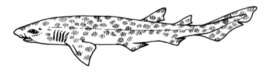

Greater spotted dogfish.

can reach weights of up to 20lb, although most weigh 10–14lb. Bull huss are reddish-brown in colour with large dark blotches. Basically nocturnal feeders, bull huss frequent the same sort of ground that

conger infest, and in deep water they can be caught during the day.

The lesser spotted dogfish lives mainly on sandy ground where it seldom reaches a weight of more than 2½lb. Similar in basic colour to a bull huss, the lesser spotted dogfish lacks the dark blotches, and instead its spots are small and neat. Both species are opportunist feeders and will take fish, squid, worm or shellfish baits. Neither species puts up much of a struggle when hooked. When handling dogfish it pays to be careful as both types have the unpleasant habit of wrapping themselves around an unwary hand or arm, and the sandpaper-like skin can cause nasty abrasions.

SPURDOG

Similar in outward appearance to the tope, the spurdog can grow to 3½–4ft in length. They should be handled with care as they have a claw-like spine at the leading edge of the dorsal fin which can cause deep cuts. Normally a pack species, spurdog make a considerable nuisance of themselves by snapping up baits intended for better fish. A single spurdog pack may contain thousands of individual fish. Unlike most other dogfish spurdog do not confine their activity entirely to the sea bed, and they can and will feed at any level between the bottom and the surface. Once a pack is located fish can be caught two or three at a time, and for this

Fig 63 By hooking the crab through the eye socket, it will remain alive for a long period.

reason they are popular with competition anglers. Ever hungry spurdog will snap up just about any bait the angler cares to offer – fresh or stale it is all the same to these voracious little sharks. Spurdog are normally found in deep water and are seldom caught by the shore fisherman.

SMOOTHOUND

Probably the hardest fighting of all the dogfish, the smoothound is very much a shallow-water species. During recent years the smoothound has become something of a cult species, popular with shore and small boat anglers alike. The adult smoothound is similar in basic appearance to the tope, but its fins tend to be a little larger. Adult fish have grey backs with white underparts. The somewhat smaller starry smoothound has a freckling of white spots on its back. Local names for the smoothound include

Smoothound are one of the most sporting of British sea fish.

Bull huss are normally found over rough ground.

Often found in large packs, spurdog provide good sport during February, March and April.

A lone angler tries his luck on the beach.

ray-mouthed dogfish and skate-toothed shark. These fish in fact do not have teeth, but their lips are armoured with bony plates like those of a skate. Smoothounds grow to weights in excess of 20lb. Very much a bottom feeder the smoothound feeds on crabs (see Fig 63), hermit crabs, worms and brittle starfish; seldom do they show interest in fish bait.

Normally caught on running ledger tackle, the smoothound is a hard fighter and the best catches are usually taken during sultry wind-free weather. It is a fussy feeder and the smoothound may play with a bait for some time before taking it firmly. On light tackle these fish are strong, dogged fighters, and nowadays most anglers tend to return each fish alive to the sea.

Glossary

Attractor spoon — Plastic or metal spoon used above baited hook to attract large fish to bait.

Bait clip — Used in uptide fishing to aid casting. The trace is doubled back so that hook and bait are hung over the clip. When tackle hits the surface the impact dislodges the hook, allowing the trace to stream out naturally with the tide.

Beads — Used as a stop between swivel and lead boom or in rows as an attraction for flatfish.

Boat-casting — To cast away from the boat, using a wired sinker to hold a position on the sea bed.

Butt pad — Special belt with metal or plastic cup to give support to rod.

Calamari squid — A type of small imported squid.

Charter boat — A large boat that takes out groups of anglers on chartered trips.

Crimp — Section of brass or copper tubing used instead of knots or wire trace.

Crimping tool — Specially designed pliers for crushing metal crimps.

Dacron — Fishing line is made from this man-made thread.

Eddystone boom — A commercially made plastic boom for wreck fishing.

Flying collar wreck boom — An L-shaped boom used especially with artificial baits.

French boom — Wire or plastic paternoster boom used for whiting and other small fish.

Gaff — Strong metal hook used to lift light fish into the boat.

Jig — Another name for a pirk.

Lead link — Sliding boom with clip to hold lead, i.e. Kilmore boom, zip slider, reel boom and the like.

Link/snap swivel — As above but with additional clip for fast release.

Mackerel feathers — Brightly dyed feathers tied to hooks, made up mainly of synthetic materials.

Muppet — Common name for an artificial squid lure.

Paternoster — A terminal tackle in which several hooks are carried on short lines attached to the main line above the sinker.

Pirk — Heavy chromed metal bar designed to simulate fish.

Plug — An artificial fish lure available in a range of sizes and weights.

Rocky beach — Consists of many rock formations surrounded by flat sand or gravel.

Rubby dubby — Minced fish, bran and fish oil used to attract sharks.

Rubby-dubby bag — Mesh bag used to hold 'dubby' hung over the side of a boat. This type of bag releases a constant trail of bait particles into the sea.

Shirvy — Groundbait made up of minced fish or meat, fish or animal blood, and bran.

Shoulder harness — Used as a support when clipped to reel lugs.

Sliding float — Float designed for use in water deeper than rod length. Fishing depth determined by section of rubber band hitched to the reel line.

Spiral link — Means of joining trace to line, yet retaining rapid release principle.

Steep to shingle beach — Drops rapidly into deep water.

Surf beach — Shallow beach exposed to prevailing winds.

Swivel — Rotating metal device for joining line or trace to line.

T-bar — Gadget for unhooking fish.

Trolling — Fishing with rod and running line and dead bait or with spoon-bait drawn behind boat.

Wander tackle — Rig for catching plaice and large dabs, incorporating two spiral leads.

Index